Wicca:

This Book Includes: Wicca For Beginners & Wicca Spells. Discover The Power of Wicca, Wiccan Spells, Herbal Magic, Essential Oils & Witchcraft Rituals

© **Copyright 2020 Sofia Visconti - All rights reserved.**

The content contained within this book may not be reproduced, duplicated, or transmitted without direct written permission from the author or the publisher.

Under no circumstances will any blame or legal responsibility be held against the publisher, or author, for any damages, reparation, or monetary loss due to the information contained within this book, either directly or indirectly.

Legal Notice:

This book is copyright protected. It is only for personal use. You cannot amend, distribute, sell, use, quote or paraphrase any part, or the content within this book, without the consent of the author or publisher.

Disclaimer Notice:

Please note the information contained within this document is for educational and entertainment purposes only. All effort has been executed to present accurate, up to date, reliable, complete information. No warranties of any kind are declared or implied. Readers acknowledge that the author is not engaging in the rendering of legal, financial, medical, or professional advice. The content within this book has been derived from various sources. Please consult a licensed professional before attempting any techniques outlined in this book.

By reading this document, the reader agrees that under no circumstances is the author responsible for any losses, direct or indirect, that are incurred as a result of the use of the information contained within this document, including, but not limited to, errors, omissions, or inaccuracies.

A SPIRITUAL START!

Start your week with gratitude, joy, inspiration, and love.

Healing, motivation, inspiration, challenge and guidance straight to your inbox every week!

FIND OUT MORE

Table of Contents

Introduction	6
Chapter 1: What is Wicca?	8
Chapter 2: History of Wicca	13
Chapter 3: Wiccan Tools & Equipment for Spells & Rituals	20
Chapter 4: Wiccan Beliefs & Traditions	33
Chapter 5: Wiccan Groups	46
Chapter 6: Witchcraft & How It Relates To Wicca	50
Chapter 7: General Wiccan Holiday Celebrations	56
Chapter 8: The Wiccan Altar	62
Chapter 9: Principles of Wicca	67
Chapter 10: Deities & The Divine	73
Chapter 11: The Wicca Elements	83
Chapter 12: Understanding Wicca Rituals	94
Chapter 13: Wicca Symbols	108
Chapter 14: Preparing For Spell Casting	112
Chapter 15: Instructions For Spell casting	118
Chapter 16: Casting Spells For The Days Of The Week	134
Chapter 17: Wicca & Magic	146
Chapter 18: Your First Steps As A Beginner In Wicca	149
Chapter 19: Casting Different Types Of Spells	154
Chapter 20: The Elements Of The Witch's Path	170

Chapter 21: The Benefits Of Wicca   179

Chapter 22: Healing Powers of Herbs & The Practice of Wicca   191

Chapter 23: Wicca & The Spirit World   199

Chapter 24: Dispelling Common Myths About Wicca   204

CONCLUSION   207

Introduction

Wicca is an English term that predominantly means "old religion". The concept of Wicca is greatly dynamic and constantly evolving, which makes it difficult to associate it with one particular meaning or definition. However, the fact that remains constant is that the Wiccan practice is an earth-centered religion which has its roots in the ancient practices of the Shaman people.

The world is full of Wiccan people who are all practicing witchcraft every day to support wholeness and wellness in their lives. There is a long history of these spells and herbal lore that will be included in this book to help you gain an understanding of where it comes from and how you have known it all along.

You will walk the path of Wicca and learn how to begin your journey of magic and mystery, working with the natural energies of all that surrounds you to bring joy, bliss, power and truth into your every day life.

This book gives a total and complete overview of what the Wiccan religion really is, of its wonderfully vast history and of the people who have sworn on their lives to protect it. Prepare to not only get a greater understanding of the faith, but also of yourself and your place in the universe.

Wicca is all about teaching you how to allow yourself patience and self-care while being able to fully work on your spiritual and physical growth. With Wicca, you can practice meditation and learn how to be self-aware while also being aware of what is around you. You can recognize what is unhealthy and make decisions to change.

Once you finish reading this book, you should be able to fully understand the basics of Wicca, including information regarding the traditions and holidays and how Witchcraft is used, and you should have a deeper understanding about yourself and how to go about becoming a Wiccan.

The time is now. Your spiritual growth is always something you should focus on. Don't be afraid of change, as you will understand in more depth if you take this path about how to be adaptable to the many changes Wicca can help you with. Whether you want to learn, grow, change certain aspects of your life, or become a full-fledged Wiccan, this book will help you decide and answer any and all questions you may have. It's time to begin your journey through the world of Wicca.

For those who are interested in entering the world of Wicca, this guide is designed to provide you with an armory of introductory spells which can be used by beginner practitioners.

It's time for you to become an amazing full-pledged Wiccan and perform magic spells to achieve whatever it is that you want in life: from true love to a steamy romance, from financial stability to riches beyond your wildest imagination.

Chapter 1: What is Wicca?

Wicca is considered to be a modern religion that is Earth-centered. Its practices and traditions are rooted in shamanic ancestry. Wiccans are the followers of the Wicca religion. Although not all Wiccans identify themselves as Pagans, it is considered to be a Pagan religion. It is important to note that Wicca as a religion is very dynamic and is always changing and it is therefore hard to give a blanket statement of its definition that will be agreeable to all its practitioners. However, the one thing that binds all Wiccans is nature. When a Wiccan observes the stars or a snowy mountain, they will feel the presence of the divine. All practitioners revere the life-sustaining and life-giving powers of nature, which are considered to be divine. Wiccans are committed to living in the balance of the earth and worship the divine nature through different rituals.

Wiccans have no centralized place of worship unlike other religions such as Christianity, Judaism, and Islam. This depicts how Wiccan traditions are decentralized as opposed to being organized. Wiccan practitioners have the freedom to choose where they would like to worship. This could happen in nature or in public spaces. In addition, Wiccans are free to choose to practice as individuals, as circles or in covens. The other thing is that there is no "holy book." Wiccans have a pantheistic view of the world in contrast to other monotheistic traditions. Wiccan practitioners hold different beliefs and notions. Some Wiccans believe in nature as the divine source with the God and the Goddess as the deities while others have additional deities.

Wiccans have the freedom to seek their own spiritual truths and path. As a tradition, Wicca is fluid and has infinite paths. The common tenet in the Wicca tradition is care and reverence for the Earth.

More than being a system of faith, Wicca is a way of life. To be Wiccan means gaining absolute appreciation and respect for life. To be Wiccan is to be one with nature. Far from claiming the title as owners of the earth, Wiccans are encouraged to accept and embrace their humble human existence. To be Wiccan is to recognize and revere the existence of greater powers. This is why when Wiccans enter the temple of their deities, they free themselves from the control of human technology.

To be Wiccan is to recognize power in everything and every creature that you behold. As Wiccan, it is for you to see the divine power in whatever face it chooses to manifest itself. That face can be in the form of the naked tree branches shivering in the autumn wind or in the promise held by each petal of a budding flower in spring.

Wiccans are peaceful, harmonious, and balanced in the way they choose to live their lives, welcoming oneness with the universe and themselves. To be Wiccan means that you are choosing to be centered with Earth. It stems from the practices of the shamanic ancestors. Wiccans believe in living in balance with nature and sustaining their powers through worship and commitment to Earth. In other words, Wicca is classified as a Pagan religion, but not all Wiccans are Pagans. It is hard to define exactly what Wicca is, because the religion and the term are both extremely complex and continually evolving.

The Life Cycles of the Wiccan Religion

The idols of Wicca are the female and male essences known as gods and goddesses. They encompass all life forms found on Earth. They are responsible for all creations involved with the circle of life and death in the universe. The gods and goddesses are worshipped throughout the year, and Wiccans host festivals for this very purpose. In most cases, Gods are worshipped or called upon in a Sabbat, and they are worshipped with the Earth's position proportionate to the sun, which includes solstices, equinoxes, and the four cross-quarter days that fall in between those solar points. The "goddesses" are mostly called upon and worshipped in the Esbat celebrations, which are worshipped every full moon.

The Religion Itself

The Wiccan religion does not follow any specific guidelines as many other religions do. They do not use any particular places to worship their gods and goddesses, such as a church, and they also do not use any official holy book like Christians. Wiccans like to worship their beliefs inside their home, in public places, or in natural settings, such as in a forest or by a river. All Wiccans are different in their practices and beliefs. For example, some Wiccans have a very universal view of the world, meaning that all sources that they need to use are provided and present in nature. The main focus of Wicca is to respect and care for the earth and all of nature, including the living things within it, such as plants, animals, and minerals.

Wicca is not a devil-worshipping religion. The devil or Satan is not a Wiccan concept and does not exist in Wiccan beliefs. Most Wiccans strive to make positive, healthy decisions throughout their lives because many believe in karma or the Rule of Three (what you give you get back three times, whether that's something good or bad). There's no fear of hell to dominate Wiccan lives; just the motivation to make an active choice to do good for the sake of releasing positive energy and doing what's right on their own accord.

Wicca is not hateful, spiteful or evil. Wiccans do not sit in darkness and make animal sacrifices; that is a myth inspired by historic misconceptions spread to deter people from pagan practices. Wiccans embrace and respect both shadow and light, death and life. Wiccan ideals are built on balance, peace and love for all living things, not malicious intent.

Anyone of any age, gender, race or background can become a Wiccan. Avoid relying on Hollywood stereotypes to make assumptions about pagans; many witches and Wiccans lead normal lives just like everyone else, with a day job, kids and bills. Not all Wiccans are "good" or "bad" people, just like not all Christians are "good" or "bad". The pagan community is extremely diverse and no one person is the same as another.

Wicca is rich with stories, rituals and beliefs. Before going into too much detail, it is important to note that the history of Wicca is surrounded by debate and controversy. The origins of Wiccan traditions and practices are hard to trace for a myriad of reasons, including the fact that Wicca is a secretive and often very personal religion.

Many traditional covens are oath-bound and do not share their practices or even the names of their gods with non-initiates. Although it is hard to pinpoint exactly when and where the old ways of paganism became Wicca, it is safe to say that it had many influences and we may never know the full extent of Wiccan history.

To fully understand Wicca, you must first understand Paganism. Paganism is any religion that is different from common world religions and has a pre-Christian belief system. Its broad definition creates a fair amount of controversy regarding the origins and factual history of this ancient Earth-based ideology. Branches of this ancient faith include Druidism, Free Masons and many others. It is also a common belief that all Christian paths of faith got their roots from Pagan ideologies and incorporated many Pagan holidays into their own belief system. Paganism, Wicca and Witchcraft are not the same thing, even though they have connections with each other.

Chapter 2: History of Wicca

Wicca as a religion dates back in history in two ways: the mythical story of it being a timeless religion that empowers human beings to connect with divinity at the core of the mystery of nature or the factual founding of the religion in the 1950s and 40s in England. The myth about Wicca goes further to state that it was a hidden tradition during the persecution of Pagans by Christians many years ago and finally safely emerged in modern times. It is this notion that makes Wicca a very attractive religion. In these modern times coupled with materialism, industrialization, and consumerism, a lot of people are yearning for a mystical practice that seems to give a sense of calm and perspective.

Gerald Gardner was born in the year 1884. As a young man, Gerald Gardner loved to travel and had a keen interest in folklore, anthropology and archaeology. These interests deepened further into occult and spiritualism. Wicca as a religion is attributed to Gerald Gardner. Being a member of several clubs that were in tandem with his diverse interests, he joined the membership of Rosicrucian Order where he was introduced to a new friend who was apparently a member of a coven of Witches. This led to his initiation in September 1920. Several years before 1920, Gardner had heard of a religion that was in existence before Christianity and was at the verge of being stamped out. He was obviously intrigued by this. Rumor had it that it was being practiced secretly in Western Europe and was being practiced in 13 member covens. According to

Margaret Murray who was an anthropologist in those days, the religion was referred to as a "Witch-cult." Obviously, Gardner made plans to meet this New Forest Group who were apparently the only group still practicing this pre-Christian old religion. He was determined to be part of them and to ensure the survival of the religion in the 20th Century.

Although Gardner was intrigued by other religions in the 1940s, the New Forest Coven deeply convinced him because of its ideas and experiences. He wound up forming his religion which he called Bricket Wood. With Bricket Wood, he began the reincarnation of the Witch-Cult, deriving ideas and inspiration from the different spiritual insights from Freemasonry, New Forest Covens, occult key figures such as Cecil Williamson and Aleister Crowley. He also derived inspiration from the elements of ceremonial initiation. In the birth of this new religion, Gardner incorporated an important aspect that became the foundation of Wicca. This was the reverence of a God and a Goddess. The two were equal to one another. This particular element was highly intriguing and unique as the society was set in patriarchal beliefs and its ways were all male-dominated.

Notably, Gardner himself never named the religion "Wicca." This name emanated from the spread of the religion to Australia and the United States in the 20th Century. During his time, the religion was called "Witchcraft" or "Old Religion" and was sometimes shortened as "the Craft." However, he sometimes called the members of his new religion "Wiccans." The Wicca according to ancient English referred to divine skilled people and sorcerers. Wicca is now currently perceived as an invention of the American people. This is because it is believed that the now Wicca religion does not actually strictly follow the Bricket Wood Coven. His earlier followers and other occultists developed other variations of the religion. The followers who practice Gardner's original traditions are widely based in the UK and call their practice the British Traditional Witchcraft. In other places around the world, however, Gardnerian Wicca is the actual practice. In the 20th Century, there were several other key figures that participated in publicizing the Witchcraft movement. They were all friends and colleagues of Gardner namely Raymond Buckland, Patricia Crowther, Doreen Valiente, Robert Cochrane, and Lois Brane. However, Gerald Gardner is recognized and respected as the father of modern Witchcraft due to his incredible efforts. This demonstrates that the Wiccan religion has an enormous history. Notably, the ideas used by Gardner to develop this religion stemmed from other older religions that were already being practiced. These traditions dated back into the revival of the British occult in the 19th century and all the way back to the 13th century. The occultists during this Middle Age period developed their ideas, knowledge and practices from ancient civilizations.

Wicca began in the early twentieth century, and it originated in England among secret covens who based their religious practices upon the research of "witch cult". Gerald Gardner was the spiritual pioneer who sought to bring this religion into existence, as he felt

Christianity was taking over society. Gardner and other spiritual explorers formed a coven and started to worship the gods and goddesses of the evolving religion. Only upon initiation were the details of this secret coven introduced to new members who were interested in the Wiccan ways.

The modern Wiccans refer to the past belief system as the "Old Religion". At first, Wicca was not a very popular practice, but over time, as old members left Gardner's practices, they formed their own covens and passed down their beliefs. The religion spread and ultimately, it began being referred to as Wicca. Wiccans are now found all the way from England to North America, and covens are scattered across the world, forming this religion's beliefs and practices.

Witchcraft was around for thousands of years before Wicca was known. In today's age, witches are known to be evil and unrighteous, but these myths originated from a few different places. From the fifteenth to the eighteenth century, lies were made about witches in order to convert followers to the church's perspectives. The goal was to make people fear the intentions of witches so as to push them away from the religion. Another misconception of Witchcraft in the early centuries involved men not understanding the physiology of women, especially their monthly cycle. Due to these misunderstandings, the unknown played a part in the church's agenda in giving the control over to the "witch hunters". As a result of this, the power of women healers was taken and handed over to male physicians.

Due to these misconceptions from the early days, the belief that witchery is horrible and disgraceful can be seen in today's culture and society. The reason Wicca was named and passed on is to replace the embarrassment, escape the persecution, and adopt the religion as a way to look at Witchcraft differently.

Wicca originates from much older pagan religions first developed in England in much earlier civilizations. These ancient pagan beliefs centered on worshipping the natural cycles of the earth. This makes a lot of sense because, before advanced technology, people had to rely on the seasons, the weather and the ever-changing biology and geology of the land for their very survival.

In 1951, Wicca BY Gerald Gardner through his books and teachings. Wicca had already been in development from pagan roots, but Gardner was one of the first people to start founding the Wicca community. To this day, Wicca continues to evolve and grow along with its practitioners.

Contrary to common knowledge, Wicca is not centuries old. It originated in the 1950s and can be traced to Gerald Gardner. In the book, he listed down and discussed various age-old Wiccan practices which were based from the ancient coven he was a member of—where the details in the book were also based on.

Even though many of the information discussed from Gardner's Wiccan book were a mix of ceremonial magic and folk practices, it is still widely believed that the Wiccan religion sprouted through his teachings and book. In fact, within the Wiccan pagan community, it is widely accepted and believed that Gardner created the Wiccan religion himself, while drawing on old pagan beliefs and ceremonial magic practices—in short, Gardner basically revived an old religion that existed way before Christianity and thus confused people into identifying the Wiccan religion with the old pagan beliefs.

In the beginning, the Wiccan religion was very coven-oriented and the only way to get to know more about the religion was to join a Wiccan coven. It was not until the late 1980's where solitary practitioner became widely pursued when Scott Cunningham published his book titled "Wicca: A Guide for the Solitary Practitioner." It was through this book that the Wiccan religion garnered a huge following through people who wanted to discover this spiritual practice without having to join a coven. And through this initiative, it has likewise opened a huge realm of Wiccan religion where individuals can find different ways of expressing the nature of their Wiccan religion.

Ever since Gerald introduced the religion to the world, it has changed in a number of ways. First, the tradition is no longer hidden and mysterious, and many people know about its existence. Therefore, if any person affirms to their various beliefs, they are likely to have an easier time joining it with absolutely no fear of persecution. Gardner also published his first book about the rituals, known as the Book of Shadows. The publication contains vital information about the practice, with spells and basic information that pertains to Wicca. Although the original idea was for the book to be a secret, it has since spread, and many people have gained access to it. Through the book, more people are privy of everything that pertains to the practice and if it appeals to them to join. To date, several versions of the publications have been published. However, it is important to note that reading the books may not really be enough to get all the vital information regarding the religion; you may need to seek out various sources to get the full picture. Since the founding witches did not really write anything down concerning their religion, the knowledge of the real history is undoubtedly a little difficult to grasp.

Gardner receives credit for not only introducing the practice to the modern world but also for also founding the current Wicca movement, which still follows the tenets of the ancient practices. The practice is no longer considered to be secret and is open to any person who may want to be a member. The current Wicca tradition is still based on the reverence of nature, performing magic and the worship of the female deity known as the goddess.

Despite the growing popularity, people from other religions continue to view Wicca in a negative light. The fact that the Wiccan describe themselves as witches is seen as Satanic, which creates a form of strife and division among them. Other religions may have difficulty even interacting with the Wiccans, as they are associated with demonic and satanic notions. Wiccans have continued to disassociate themselves with devil worship, although it is not easy. The Wiccans will often say that it is easier for them to associate with Hindus and other religions which are nature-oriented, as opposed to most religions which are deity-oriented.

Chapter 3: Wiccan Tools & Equipment for Spells & Rituals

Before casting any spells, you must first familiarize yourself with the basic tools used in spell casting and in performing rituals. Each Wiccan tool is rich with meaning. Some Wiccan tools are living beings plucked from nature's womb, but it is important to understand that as Wiccan, you are entitled to only take what is willing. Remember, each time you harvest a plant or use a crystal for your spell, you are asking that living being to sacrifice its life for you. In the end, you must make sure that your intention is worthy of their lives.

Wiccans typically have altars that they use for rituals and ceremonies. The altar is actually an important focal point in their rituals. It does not really matter that much if it is elaborate or simple. So, you can tailor your altar according to your personal preference. You also do not have to spend too much money on it. You can simply use the materials that you already have in your home. Remember that it is not the appearance of your altar that counts, but rather the way you use it.

You can use a fixed altar if you have one. You can also use a folding table if you live in a small home and do not have a lot of space. Folding tables are great because you can easily fold and store them away after you use them. There is no single rule for decorating an altar. A variety of tools, clothing, and jewelry may be used. It is up to your discretion whether you will use these tools or not. You should go with whatever feels comfortable for you. Nevertheless, there are certain items that are recommended to be used for your altar.

Wicca incorporates the use of various tools and elements in its activities and practices. Wiccan tools are many, and they are used to achieve focus and a direct spiritual connection due to the main purpose of facilitating the connection with the divine and spiritual energy. Through the use of specific tools and symbols, the Wiccan believe that they can be used to harness and direct the co-creative force, ultimately welcoming the desired energies and deities to perform any magical tasks desired.

The exact number of tools used by the Wiccans is unknown, as it varies with the traditions of the specific group, as well as with the spells that the group mostly casts. Some traditions use very complex tools, while others only use the simplified ones available to them. Wicca is a practice that has always use somewhat complex tools. The tools are not really mandatory, and they are not used by all witches. However, their utilization is associated with a better connection to the energies and a higher chance of achieving success therein. The list of the tools involved in the various spells is exhaustive. The following are the most commonly used tools for the spells and rituals done in Wiccan traditions:

Wand

This tool is actually optional. You can choose to have a wand or not. You can buy it from a store or have it custom made. If you choose to have a wand, you can refer to various traditions. In general, a wand has to be the length of your elbows, fingers, and hand but it can also be twice or half its size. You can choose any material for your wand, but woods are more ideal because they are used by ancient Druids. They are also more connected to nature.

Athame and Sword

An athame is a small knife typically made with wood. It is basically a mini dagger. A sword, on the other hand, is much bigger. It generally comes in a variety of sizes and shapes and is bigger than an athame. You can choose whatever athame or sword best fits your personal preferences. Nonetheless, it is ideal for your athame to be double ended. It also has to have a dark wood on its handle. If you want to personalize it, you can carve symbols on its handle.

Boline

This one is also a knife. It has a white handle and a curved blade. It is mainly used to cut sacred items that have to be used for rituals and ceremonies. When you use a boline, see to it that you are careful so that you can avoid accidents. You can order this tool online or buy it from a store that sells garden supplies.

Besom

It is a broom that is used in the cleaning process during a ritual. However, you do not necessarily have to sweep the floor. You can use this tool for a symbolic purpose. When you choose a bosom, see to it that you go for something that is made with natural materials. If you cannot find a besom from a store, you can make your own. Depending on which Wiccan coven or group you belong to, you should follow certain specifications when making your own besom.

Chalice

It is a container used to contain wine, fruit juice, or any other liquid needed for a ritual. You can find chalices in numerous sizes and shapes. Generally, a chalice is simply a cup with a long stem, similar to that of a wine glass. You can get a chalice that is made from any material. Glass and brass are the most commonly used materials for chalices.

Bell

It is used to attract positive energies and invoke deities during rituals. Bells come in different sizes and shapes. They are also widely available, so you can easily purchase them from anywhere. It is up to what kind of bell you will use for your altar. You can use a small one or a big one. You may prefer a small bell since it is easier to hold and has a mild tone. This is especially ideal if you live in a condo or apartment unit and do not want to disturb your neighbors during rituals.

Incense

In a similar fashion, where a candle might bring light and warmth, incense is able to bring scent and aura. Throughout this guide, there will be times when you may need to burn incense. There are several ways in which to go about this, so the best advice is to simply use the method that is most familiar to you. Often it is not the way in which the incense is burned, but the act of burning itself that is important. This means that you can have a variety of options. As well as this, the various flavors and brands of incense often come down to the personal preferences of the practicing witch, so it can help to find the types which you are most comfortable with in order to create the best possible aura.

Offering bowl

While this might seem like one of the more magical objects, an offering bowl is simply a tried and tested place in which you can offer up your ingredients in a designated place. Sometimes, the bowls are fireproof and designed to hold burning materials. If you are using them for such purposes, be sure to check beforehand whether they are actually fireproof.

A type of ritual knife which is used by many witches, these come in all shapes and sizes. Many people often have a specially designated knife for different types of spell. While not always sharp, many witches find that their magic flows better when their magical knives have been properly sharpened. These should not be used for general household chores.

Oils

Throughout this guide, you may occasionally see references and calls to use aromatic oils. There are a huge range of these oils, and much like incense, certain types can often be tied to certain spells and types of magic and energy. If you are required to make use of an oil relevant to yourself or to another person, then it can be important to be sure that you are picking the right one. With hundreds of options available, it can be worth dedicating time to getting this selection right, with the aromatic properties providing different uses.

Various household items

At certain points and during certain spells, you may need to use items which are usually found around the home. This could be anything from a potted plant, to sea salt, to a piece of string or even just a glass of water. In these instances, it can be possible to use standard, non-magical items. Even those items which are just laying around the home will have their own personal and private energies and these can be turned towards a better use through the practice of Wicca. As a practical and natural magic, Wicca has a long history of incorporating the everyday and turning it into the magical. As such, do not be surprised to see even the most mundane object become magical when used in the correct manner.

Cauldron

This tool is perhaps the most associated one with Wicca. It is used to stir and combine ingredients that are used in rituals. As with many of the tools placed on altars, you can find cauldrons in various sizes and shapes. However, you do not have to put your cauldron on your altar if it is too big and heavy. Cauldrons are basically iron pots that have large bottoms and three legs. If your altar is small, you may get a small cauldron that does not take up much space.

Crystal Ball

This tool is used to represent the Goddess. Wiccans gaze into their crystal ball to have a vision. You can find crystal balls in different sizes and types. However, once you acquire a crystal ball, make sure that you charge it magically as soon as you can. Crystal balls have long been used in witchcraft and other similar practices.

Sensor

This tool is used to hold the incense that you burn during your rituals. You can find sensors in different sizes, shapes, and materials. They are typically made of brass. Nonetheless, you may also use a hanging sensor or a glass tray if it is more convenient for you. A hanging sensor is actually ideal if you wish to disperse the smoke from your incense during your ritual sessions.

Altar Tile

This tool is used as the central area during the ritual process and may contain a pentagram. It is available in different materials. Your altar tile can be of any size, but it is better to have one that fits your altar perfectly. You can also choose to have symbols engraved on it if you want. If your altar tile has a pentagram, see to it that it points upward, not downward.

Clothing

You are allowed to wear whatever you want during a ritual, provided that it is approved of by the members of your coven. If you are a solitary practitioner, you can wear whatever you want as long as you feel comfortable in it. You should be able to easily stand up, sit down, and move around. Most wiccans wear robes that feature embroidery, hoods, and flared sleeves. If you are not comfortable wearing a robe, you can wear something casual such as a pair of jeans and a t-shirt. You can even be nude if you like.

Jewelry and Accessories

The use of jewelry and accessories is open to many different interpretations. Wiccans are not really required to wear jewelry during a ritual. However, if you wish to wear any celestial symbol or an amulet, you can wear it. You may also wear a bracelet or a ring that features a special gem or stone.

Crystals and Stones

Crystals and Stones are symbols of the natural element Earth. When used in spells and rituals, they represent the North. They are usually used in healing spells. Sometimes, they are used as foundations for pagan altars.

Crystals are living beings which radiate vibration and are capable of lifting your own vibration simply by being within close proximity to your body. Crystals can be combined with a number of self-help and healing practices for better results. Some areas where they are finding more usage are in meditation, Feng Shui, prayer beads, home or office decoration, energy healing, amulets, baths, fertility and birth, sleep, jewelry, and massage therapy among others. Through all these uses of crystals, their link to health benefits is helpful to humans as well as animals such as your pets and plants too.

Crystals are as valuable as they are numerous. The wide varieties of crystals available today makes it possible for a lover of crystals to choose from a range of options. The good thing about crystals is that you can enjoy their health benefits regardless of how you use them. Whether you soak them in your bath water, soak them in the water you drink, wear them as ornaments or amulets, place them in a strategic corner of your room or office, put them under your pillow, or hold them while you meditate, you will always get the same health benefits that crystals are known for when you use them correctly. Normally, each kind of crystal will radiate a particular type of energy that corresponds to and works with the specific energies in certain emotional and physical areas of yourself. Using crystals for healing is as simple as being around them. Other techniques may include holding a crystal in your hand or placing it on a nightstand.

Since these healing crystals are constantly absorbing negative energy in order to provide healing, they can become blocked. Blockages will then reduce the healing effects of the crystals, hence the importance to cleanse them.

Herbs

Another natural tool that symbolizes the North is ***Herbs***. Even though they come from the earth, when used for spells, each herb may represent a different natural element.

Book of shadows

The ***Book of Shadows*** is a valuable workbook that every Wiccan should have. In some Wiccan families, the Book of Shadows contain knowledge, spells, and anecdotes-wisdom passed on from one generation to the next. You can create your own book of shadows to record your personal experiences and to keep your notes. While there are modern Wiccans who keep their spells in their computers and other smart portable devices, ultimately, a handwritten notebook is still best. After all, when you write, you are transferring the energy behind your intent into the paper, thus lending more power to your spells.

The Book of Shadows is among the most vital tools in Wicca because it contains the spells and rituals that you have to use. It is also the book that the coven turns to during rituals. As you have read, you can either have the book handwritten or computerized. Then again, handwritten is better because it lets you put your energy onto the words that you write. Your energy flows from your body to your hand to your pen and to your paper. A lot of Wiccan traditions also prefer that their members write their Book of Shadows by hand.

If you are new to Wicca, you can use the Book of Shadows of your coven as a guide when writing your own. You can also simply copy its contents so that your book will be uniform with the rest of the members of your coven. Writing your own Book of Shadows allows you to customize your spells and personalize its contents. However, see to it that you still abide by the general guidelines of Wiccan rituals and traditions.

When you write your own Book of Shadows, you also have to see to it that you use an empty book. If you do not have an empty book, you can use empty sheets of paper and bind them together. You can use any material for your Book of Shadows, although it is highly recommended that you use sturdy materials to prevent it from being damaged easily.

Candles

Candles are very common in the Wiccan practices and are used in almost all ceremonies and for the casting of spells. Candles are usually symbolic of the presence of the gods and goddesses, as well as a representation of the element of fire. The theory associated with candles is that they can be used to absorb all of the energy that is unwanted and expel any energy that you wish to get rid of. For instance, when you carry out a banishing spell, the candles will absorb all of the energy that you are trying to get rid of and attract the positive energy that you seek. Some of the Wiccan enthusiasts believe that when you make your own candles, they are more powerful compared to those that are bought in shops.

Keep in mind that you should cleanse all tools before their use. The cleansing is always conducted by mixing pure water with a little bit of sea salt and washing off the tools.

Chapter 4: Wiccan Beliefs & Traditions

Wicca is a guilt-free religion. A lot of people may think that guilt suggests you have regret, remorse, and act in a righteous manner. However, guilt and shame have nothing to do with any of that. Virtuous behavior does not come from the regret of what you have done in the past but from learning from your mistakes and choosing the right choices for your future. It is only when we learn from our actions and mistakes that motivation to become and do better is when you can love a virtuous life. The main difference between religion and spirituality is that in most religions, righteousness and morality are forced. Spirituality helps people find their own morality and righteousness within themselves and then try to live up to their own expectations. Wicca is a spiritual religion, which is to say that it is not just based upon religion or that it is purely spiritual. It is not about morality or virtuousness, it is more about the guidance that comes from the gods and goddesses and holding that within your beliefs as a Wiccan.

The spiritual truths in Wicca are as follows:

- Be your authentic true self.

- Harm nothing and no one (living things such as plants, animals, and humans).

- Whatever you put out into the universe you will get three times over (the Rule of Three).

- What you push away will continue to haunt you.

- How you think and feel creates your reality and what you go through.

- We are all equal and one.

These principles in Wicca are the source of their morality. They respect all life forms and take full responsibility for all their actions. Unlike most religions, Wiccans do not create rules, because rules can easily be broken and are hard to follow at most. So the purity of just accepting yourself is what a Wiccan stands for - learning from your mistakes and striving to always do better than you did before. They focus on seeing people as who they are and who want to be rather than focusing on who they were or used to be.

The Goddess and God

Wicca involves the worship of a God and Goddess. These figures can be viewed and interpreted in a variety of ways, but they are traditionally represented as duo-theistic deities both equal and opposite in nature. They are generally seen as a unified couple, although in some cases the God is seen as the Goddess's son (this is based on the cycles of the seasons).

The Goddess is central to the Wiccan religion. While both the God and the Goddess are worshipped, the Goddess is recognized as the creator of all. She gives birth to the Earth itself as well as the gods. The idea that motherhood and matriarchy are central to life and therefore focused on in every ritual and observance is believed to have been carried forward from ancient times until present.

There is a tangible joy, a sense of relief for many Wiccans when they come into the fold and realize that the love of the Goddess is 100% unconditional. Many Wiccans were raised in Christian households, and perhaps didn't have the loving support they were after within their family's faith. In Wicca as well as in other pagan religions, the Goddess means safety, support, never-ending healing and love. She will never abandon her children, and we are all her children, even the God.

Because the Goddess exists in all things, life must be understood as sacred and precious. This is why the Wiccan Rede is so important.

Wiccan Traditions

When it comes to practices, basically many of the Wiccan religions practice all or some of the traditions listed below.

- Being a part of a coven, unless they are a solitary Wiccans
- Worships a goddess or god, or several of them
- Practices witchcraft or magic
- Honors the seasons or nature
- Celebrates 8 Sacred days each year, known as the Sabats

Depending on the Wiccan denomination that you would want to join or belong, they may have some unique traditions particular to their faith. But, generally these are the traditions of the Wiccan religion.

The Rule of Three

Also called the Threefold Law, the Rule of Three states that whatever you send into the world will eventually return to you, triple the amount. It serves to remind us that for every action there is a reaction, and that we should never be careless with our power, intentions, or magic. The world certainly needs as much benevolence as it can get, so if we have to choose between reactions of love and patience and reactions of malice or rage, we should strive to choose the former, and abstain from the latter with as much strength as we possess. The Rule of Three or Three-fold Law states that "You get back the energy you put into the world three times over". Whatever you do will come back to you later on, whether that's a positive or negative thing.

In essence, if you make positive choices, help others and contribute something good to the world, you will enjoy three times the positivity and happiness in return. Alternatively, if you release negativity and do bad things, bad things will come back to you. Again, not everyone follows or believes in the Rule of Three.

The Wiccan Rede

The Wiccan Rede has many forms, but usually states "An it harm none, do what ye will". More clearly, it reads "As long as you harm none, do what you will". Not all Wiccans follow the Wiccan Rede, but many use the Rede as a statement of morality to help guide choices in life. The Rede doesn't necessarily mean that we can all do whatever we want as long as we don't hurt others; it's more about making the choice to avoid harming others, both physically and emotionally, and living life to the fullest. In other words, you are responsible for your actions. The exact meaning of the Rede is often debated among different Wicca communities. Spend some time meditating on the concept of the Rede and interpret it as you see fit based on your personal preferences and morals. The general idea is that you actively make choices that are good and moral, but you also have pure freedom to live your life as you choose.

There are a few different variations on this, but they all mean the same thing: you have the free will to make your own choices, but please try to make choices that will not directly, negatively effect another person. Make sure your intention is benevolent, even in matters of banishment and protection.

This is why the Words of Casting are used to close every spell. These state that "By the power of three times three, I cast this spell and set it free—to do no harm, nor to bring any harm to me, I cast this spell, so may it be."

Moon Phases for Spells

The moon is a great governess to the workings of Wiccan ritual. She has her phases and moves from dark to light and then back to dark again. The moon represents an important cycle that happens every month of the year and will always happen as long as the Earth spins and she orbits.

Working with moon magic is a daily part of Wicca. Having a moon calendar handy to acquaint yourself with the phases of the moon is a good practice as well as understanding the aspects of the moon and what she represents through her phases. Calling upon moon energy in your rituals and practices is an important part of the experience.

Many practitioners with perform rituals only on the new and full moons while others will focus on the first and last quarter moons as well. The moon pulls the tides and affects the seasons. She governs how things grow just as much as the sun does. She pulls your waters within just as she pulls the waters of the world.

Moon rituals are a huge factor of Wiccan spiritual beliefs and practices so find out what phase of the moon you are in today and look into exactly what that means for you and your practices.

You can also make use of the power of the moon phases to make your spell more potent.

Waning Moon

When the begins to grow small each night going into the dark of the new moon all over again is the perfect time for removing things in your life. The waning moon is best used for ending relationships, breaking addictions, and banishing bad habits.

Full Moon

Of all moon phases, the full moon is the easiest to identify. The full moon lasts only for a short time when compared to waning and waxing moon phases. In order to make use of the power of the full moon, do try to make use of its energy in between the two days before and two days after the actual full moon. The full moon is best used for making difficult choices, divination, psychic talents, romance, fertility, love, and anything creative or artistic.

Waxing Moon

The waxing moon is when the moon begins to get bigger before becoming a full moon. During this time, growth and development is best explored. The waxing moon is best used for general good luck, healing, friendships, inspiration, motivation, and personal strength.

New Moon

The new moon marks the beginning of the lunar cycle and is lined up with the positions of both the earth and the sun. The sky is dark and you cannot actually see the moon. At this time, this is most powerful beginnings. The new moon is best used for new career opportunities, personal improvement, health, beauty, and beginnings of any kind.

Seasonal Ritual and Rite of Passage

The witch's calendar year is full of holidays and rituals that celebrate the seasons as they begin. Usually coordinating on specific full moon or new moon cycles, these seasonal rituals are a major part of how Wiccans celebrate nature ant the seasons and cycles of life. The principle of honoring the rites of passage through time is a big part of Wicca. They occur at the beginning of a season or the end of a cycle to help you prepare for what is ahead in accordance with the natural cycles of Mother Earth.

Many people have specific rituals and rites of passage that they practice at these times of the year and they usually involve very specific herbs, elemental ceremonies, and a god or goddess who represents the time of year.

Following along with the seasonal shifts and living life through the rhythms of the Earth is a part of Wiccan culture and practice and the belief in the seasons and cycles as a reflection of life is of vital importance.

What Makes a Wiccan Unique

There are defining attributes of Wiccans:

- Wiccans practice rituals in order to live according to the rhythm of nature. These are observed as the Lunar phases, the equinoxes, the solstices, and the other Sabbaths.

- Wiccans realize that human intelligence comes with a responsibility towards one's environment, therefore, Wiccans try to live in harmony with nature, with practices that benefit the environment and the evolution of all life.

- Wiccans acknowledge the fact that through the practice of magic, they possess a power that is greater than most average persons. Although it may be called a "supernatural" ability by some, Wiccans propose that is is actually part of the natural world, merely overlooked by non-practitioners.

- Wiccans recognize the duality of the Universe as possessing both masculine and feminine, similar to the concepts of Yin and Yang. Neither is greater than the other; they are supportive and necessary to one another, and also exist in all humans. Wiccans look at sex and sexuality as a gift from the Goddess, and not as something to be ashamed of, so long as mutual consent is given. Sex is also a divine act and a symbol of life itself.

- Wiccans recognize different planes of existence, such as the material world and the spirit world.

- Wiccans do not allow an absolute hierarchy within their ranks, but they honor the teachers, elders, priests and priestesses who give their time and devote their lives to teaching future generations the Old Ways.

- Wiccans view their practice as combining magic, religion, and nature-based wisdom. Together these elements form the Wiccan way of life.

- A witch is such because he or she practices witchcraft, not because of lineage or false claims. Degrees and initiations are the individual's choice, but they do not determine who is a witch and who is not. A witch strives to control forces within his or herself in order to live a better life, and in greater harmony with the natural world.

- Wiccans believe in seeking fulfillment and affirmation in their lives by seeking to give greater meaning to the Universe and by examining their individual roles within that Universe.

- Wiccans keep no animosity towards Christianity, save for the fact that Christianity insists it is the only "true" religion, and all others are false. Wiccans have no issue with other faiths, so long as those faiths do not strive to suppress the religious freedom of others.

- Wiccans resist feeling threatened by other members of the Craft engaging in debate about the tenets or practices of

Wicca. They welcome dialogue that seeks to further the cause of Wiccan and pave the way for the future.

- Wiccans refute the idea of "absolute evil" and do not worship entities like "Satan" or "the Devil" as defined by Christian principles. Wiccans abhor the search for power via the suffering of others.

- Wiccans believe that everything we need in life can be found in Nature and its mysteries.

Wiccan Paths

An important aspect of the Wiccan faith to understand is the fact that there is no set way to advance in one's magical education. There are opportunities to join a formal training circle as well as the option to remain practicing as a solitary witch, or any combination of the two. Many covens offer a formal education as an option to all new members. The training is presided over by a priest or priestess, and moves slowly compared to most modern schools are trades houses. The rule of thumb is to allow the aspirant to advance to the next level of knowledge after a "year and a day", which of course is dependent on how well the witch is mastering the concepts taught to them. There is no pressure or rigid timeline, because magic is not something to be taken lightly. Unlike formal education in the mundane world, it's more important to fully absorb the knowledge than it is to advance to the next level.

The goal of a formal Wiccan training is to one day achieve the coveted spot of high priest or priestess. Rather than having power over the community, these titles instead have the honor over presiding naming ceremonies, hand-fasting's, and cronings and sagings, as well as Sabbaths and esbats. Priests and priestesses are considered helpers of the God and the Goddess, and give their service to the community in sacrifice for the benefit of all, rather than being esteemed or "higher" than any one community member. A priest or priestess must never abuse their power to influence someone else, but they are often turned to for advice, and will never turn any witch away who is seeking answers to questions.

One of the reasons it's useful for a solitary witch to occasionally celebrate a Sabbath or esbat with a larger, public community or coven is the opportunity to network and talk with other witches. There's a lot to learn, and endless amounts of different insights to consider. Many large, established covens open their doors to solitary witches as long as they know another member of the coven. There is never a push to recruit a witch; joining a coven is strictly voluntary.

Wiccan Ceremony

One of the ceremonies of Wicca is something called a "Wiccaning". It is typically when a couple first has a new baby in their life, but it can occur at any age. A wiccaning serves to introduce a person by name to the members of a Wiccan community. It is neither an endorsement of the Craft nor a promise that the person being named will join the Old Ways. It can be an introduction to the child or older person's actual name, or a Wiccan name that the child or older person has picked for themselves. Wiccans believe that children are not mature enough to choose their faith, even though they may be curious about their parents' religion, and may choose to join in community celebrations happily.

Dedication

When a person does decide to enter the Craft, however, there is usually a ceremony called simply a "dedication". The person may choose a "craft name", something unique to them and known only to other members of the coven or community. Dedications are often performed at the Imbolc sabbath, when life is new and hope is in the air for the coming Spring.

Hand-fasting

When a Wiccan couple chooses to join together, they may opt to partake in a ceremony called "hand-fasting". This is not a formal marriage, although the couple may also choose to visit a judge or clerk of court to make the union official in the eyes of the law. At a hand-fasting, a priest or priestess oversees the ceremony, and loosely binds cords over the couples' clasped hands and says that they will remain together "so long as their love shall last".

Hand-parting

Hand-parting is a respectful ceremony performed if a couple decides they are no longer to be together. The cords are ritually cut with an athame or boline, and some couples choose to keep the pieces as a reminder of their time together. In Wicca, there is no stigma about a relationship ending. It is merely considered the natural course of each other's particular paths.

Croning and Saging

Croning, for women, and Saging, for men, is a way to honor the elder members of the Wiccan community. Elders are beloved in Wicca, for they are the ones who've gone on before the rest of the community to learn, teach, and light the way for future generations.

Sometimes younger members of the community undergo a croning or saging ceremony, usually when they are enduring a serious injury or illness such as cancer. Such battles mature a person well before their time, and saging and croning is a way to both pay respect to the person, and preparing them for the inevitability and peace of death, if it comes earlier than expected.

Chapter 5: Wiccan Groups

By this time, you already have a good idea on what Wicca is all about and how you can cast spells for different purposes. You have also learned about the different phases of the moon and which spells are most effective to be done during these periods.

However, before you can be a full Wiccan, you have to be initiated into a coven. During the initiation ceremony, a High Priest or a High Priestess will anoint you as a member. However, if you do not want to belong to any coven or group, you can be a solitary Wiccan. You can do a self-dedication ritual to anoint yourself to be a full Wiccan.

Initiation is a vital aspect of Wicca because it symbolizes rebirth. From the time you were initiated into it, you dedicate your whole self to the gods and goddesses. If you wish to be a High Priest or High Priestess in the future, you need to achieve a Third Degree ranking. You can do this by studying more about the religion and gaining more experiences.

Wicca is classified into different groups or covens with different traditions. Before you get initiated, however, you have to research about the different Wiccan groups so that you can gain a better understanding of them. Once you learn more about them, you can decide on which group you want to join. The following are the most well-known Wiccan groups:

Alexandrian Wicca

It was formed by Alex and Maxine Sanders. It puts emphasis on the polarity of the male and female genders. It involves rites that are dedicated to the God and the Goddess. The members of the coven usually meet during full moons and new moons, as well as Sabbats. If you want to join this Wiccan group, you have to begin as a neophyte and then move on to the First Degree.

British Traditional Wicca

It is known for their lineage, practice, and teachings. This Wiccan tradition has covens in many parts of the world. If you want to be part of this group, you have to be formally initiated by a lineage member.

Blue Star Witchcraft

The members of this group are referred to as Witches rather than Wiccans. Unlike most Wiccan groups, however, it has five levels of initiation. If you want to be a member, you have to be initiated and pass all the levels.

Circle Sanctuary

It is a non-profit religious organization that was founded in 1974 by Selena Fox. It uses networking to promote itself. The members hold events, such as the Pagan Spirit Gathering, on a regular basis.

Covenant of the Goddess

It was formed in the 1970's. Just like the British Traditional Wicca, it has different covens in different parts of the world. The members have annual conferences wherein they educate other people, perform rituals, and participate in outreach programs. They also encourage other people to know Wicca and witchcraft better by correcting the common misconceptions about the religion. They even give scholarships and legal support to the people who qualify.

Dianic Wicca

It was founded by Zsuzsanna Budapest. In the past, it only accepted women as members. Today, however, it has started accepting men as members in order to give polarity to the coven. Although the members honor both the God and the Goddess, they tend to spend more time with the Goddess. They celebrate the eight Sabbats. They also allow the practice of negative magic, such as hexing, cursing, and binding, to anyone that harms women.

Eclectic Wicca

It refers to NeoWiccan traditions that do not fall under any category. There are covens and solitary Wiccans who follow an eclectic path. Wiccans who modify or have various traditional beliefs are also called eclectic. Likewise, those who make their own traditions are also called eclectic.

Gardnerian Wicca

It was founded in the 1950s by Gerald Gardner. The members do not recruit new members, however. So, if you want to join the group, you have to be initiated. You also have to take an oath that you will never disclose to anyone outside of the coven whatever you experience within the coven. If you join this group, you will only be allowed to copy the Book of Shadows if you passed the initiation.

Seax Wicca

It was founded in 1973 by Raymond Buckland and was based on Saxon Paganism. It is a democratic group that allows members to elect their High Priest or High Priestess, as well as modify traditional rituals and practices. Seax Wicca does not involve any initiation rites. If you want to be part of it, you do not have to be initiated or do anything else. You simply have to dedicate yourself to its path.

Chapter 6: Witchcraft & How It Relates To Wicca

Are the Two Related?

There really isn't much of a difference at all between the two. In some instances, those that follow either Alexandrian or Gardernerian traditions are considered to be following the Wiccan path as opposed to those who are solo or eclectic practitioners who are considered to be practicing witchcraft.

It can be said that Wicca is more of a religion than witchcraft is. Wiccans do worship deities, witches, on the other hand, do not necessarily have to - they can even be atheists if they want to. A witch does not necessarily have to be a Wiccan and so they will not necessarily adhere to the Wiccan Rede.

The term, Wicca, does, however, contain less negative connotations than the word witchcraft and this can often be the primary reason for making a distinction. Other than that, the two are largely interchangeable.

Another distinction can be that the Wiccan path follows a more natural root - making more use of sympathetic magic and that practitioners of witchcraft follow a more arcane root - making use of extensive ritualistic magic.

Choose whichever name appeals to you - be a practitioner of Wicca or witchcraft, both paths are intertwined and lead to the same place in the end. In both traditions, the aim is to increase your knowledge and understanding of the natural world.

Different Traditions

Witchcraft or Wicca draws on a number of different traditions and the extent to which these traditions are followed largely depends on the individual or the coven. In some covens, there is a more formal structure of initiations and degrees of initiation. Some are more a lot more relaxed and eclectic in the way things are done.

Witchcraft has been around in some form or another for thousands of years and has been subject to much scrutiny, good and bad, throughout that time. It has risen and fallen in popularity, sometimes being completely demonized and at other being considered a necessary part of living.

Witchcraft is the practice of magic involving spells and invocations; not all witchcraft is Wiccan. Witchcraft can be seen in a wide range of different religions and cultures. While someone may refer to themselves as a Wiccan and witch interchangeably, Wicca and witchcraft are NOT the same thing. Witchcraft is a core component of Wicca, but there are also many witches who are not Wiccan at all.

In Ancient Egypt, for example, what was termed as black magic was illegal. At the same time though, there were several spells and magical rites that the pharaoh had to perform in order to keep the evil forces at bay.

In the Medieval era, witchcraft was pretty much completely demonized. It was still performed in secret and under the guise of folk lore but the Medieval witch was literally taking their lives into their own hands - there was no tolerance for witchcraft back then and you could be accused of committing witchcraft by anyone.

In fact, it is a commonly held belief that many people found that they could settle scores by denouncing their enemies as witches.

It was customary to get the witch to confess through the use of torture and, if that didn't work, there were trials set forth in the Malleus Maleficarum - "The Witches Hammer" that would be able to determine whether or not a person was a witch or not.

One such trial involved tying a stone to the suspected witches' feet and throwing them in a river. If they floated they were considered a witch and burned at the stake. If they drowned, their names were cleared. Clearly, it was a flawed system and led to the deaths of many people - practitioners and non-practitioners alike.

In modern times, Hollywood has dithered between witches being benevolent beings, such as those in programs like "Bewitched" and "Charmed" and witches being completely evil such as those seen in programs like "Supernatural".

In general, though, we do seem to be moving away from the stereotypical old hag dressed in black with a funny pointy hat and riding on a broomstick towards a more balanced view that witches look just like everyone else.

Are Witches Devil-Worshippers?

This is one of the abiding myths that seems to be really hard to shake off. The truth of the matter is that witches do not believe that there is a devil or even that there is a hell. You personally are responsible for what you do.

Is There No Punishment for Witches? If there is no hell, then there is no punishment, right? Well, it is a bit more complicated than that. First off, witches have a different version of what sin actually is.

Sin is a bit of a grey area in witchcraft because there are no absolutes. As a society, we tend to want to label everything - white magic and black magic, good witches and evil witches - in witchcraft though, there is no real distinction. Magic is magic, is it neither good nor bad. It is the intention with which the magic is used that is either good or bad.

An "evil" witch can thus cast spells to the good and a "good" witch can thus cast spells to the bad. That is why it is so important to approach spell-casting with the right intentions and to consider the overall effects.

By the same token though, a witch may be held to a much higher standard - instead of a standard set of rules, as set out in most religions, witches adhere to the principle that whatever you do, good or bad, will be magnified and visited on you.

So lie, cheat and steal, if you want to but just remember, you will have the same done to you many times over.

Chapter 7: General Wiccan Holiday Celebrations

Becoming a Wicca is easy and there are basically no set of rules that you have to follow. What you need to do is to essentially know more and read more about the Wiccan religion and its practices. Basically, all Wiccans live by the rule "Harm None."

- Faith is Personal – despite the fact that you worship or work within a coven, but you still connect to the god or goddess you are worshipping on a personal level. You are accountable for understanding, building, and maintaining your relationship with your god or goddess.

- The Reality of Magic – as a central part of the Wiccan philosophy, they believe that magic does exist and it forms part of their religious framework. However, not all Wiccans practice spell work and spell works can be done in varying degrees.

- The Divine is Dual – One of the central tenets of Wicca is the firm belief that the divine is both male and female, just like the duality (male/female) of nature.

The 8 Sabats

Yule (Around December 21)

This is a common celebration even for non-pagans, which they call Christmas. This is the first Sabat celebrated in the Wiccan calendar that marks the winter solstice. This is the time when the day is at its shortest. The meaning behind Yule is the rebirth of the sun, which is also why Christians mark this day as the birth of Jesus.

Yule is also known as Saturnalia and Winter Solstice. Preferred foods served in celebration of Yule are apples, baked squash, stolen, gingerbread, Yule log cakes, and cider or wassail. Common activities and traditions observed during this time are hanging mistletoe, lighting candles, giving gifts, lighting a Yule log, decorating a tree, and giving gifts.

Imbolc (February 2)

This is the first sacred day to commemorate the coming of spring. Even though there is still snow on the ground, this day heralds the first days of getting fresh food in the form of milk from ewes and other livestock after a long winter.

This day is also sacred to Brigid, who is a Celtic goddess. Offerings were left outside and cloths left on Imbolc night were believed to be blessed by the goddess which can be used later in the year for healing.

At this time, a common activity was to anticipate the coming of spring by predicting the weather which is also celebrated in non-Pagan religions, the Groundhog Day. Other names for this celebration, aside from Groundhog Day are Oimelc, Brigid's Day, and Candlemas.

Preferred foods to be served in celebrating this day are pumpkin seeds, butter, cabbage, potato soup, lamb stew, yogurt, and custard. Customary activities and traditions done during the day are lighting candles, weather predictions, lighting a bonfire, spring cleaning, and making a woven cross or bed for Brigid.

Ostara (approximately on March 21)

This is the time that coincides with the spring equinox here the day is equally long as the night. The exact date usually changes from the 22nd to the 20th year after year where it heralds the time when the days become longer than the nights. And coinciding with this time of the year, many animals are being born and the traditional farmstead would be alive with newborns. It is believed that this is behind the Easter story of Christianity punctuated by bunnies and eggs.

The Ostara is also known by other names like Alban Eiler, Lady Day, and the Spring equinox.

Preferred foods to be served in celebrating this Sabat are hot cross buns, leafy greens, strawberries, lamb, and anything with eggs. Customary traditions and activities done during the day are trying to get pregnant, beginning new projects, decorating with spring flowers, coloring or dyeing eggs.

Beltane (May 1)

Beltane is not celebrated for any specific seasonal occasion; however it is observed for sexuality, love, and life reasons. This is the time wherein summer is beginning to start which signifies it as a holiday of happiness, growth, and fertility. Due to the sexual overtones of this Sabat, it was largely frowned upon by the church and hence the reason why this day is often linked with witchery.

Preferred foods on this occasion are May wine with strawberries and woodruff, fresh baked bread, anything with honey, strawberries, and mead. The usual activities and traditions done on this day are fairy magic, picking wildflowers, jumping bonfires, braiding flower chains, sex, dancing, outdoor bonfires, and dancing ribbons around a May pole.

Litha (around June 21)

Litha is celebrated during the longest day of the year or at the height of summer which corresponds between June 20 and 22 of a given year. It marks the start of the other half of the year where the nights become longer than the days. This day is also believed to be the magickal peak day. So, if you are a practicing witch this is an important day for harvesting your herbs for plant rituals that you will be doing until the next Litha comes. This is also the best time for doing spells with herbs because it is believed that the fairy realm is quite strong during this day. Also any rituals or spells that communicated with the fairy realm will be quite strong during Litha too.

Litha is also known in other names like Whitsun, Summer solstice, or Midsummer Preferred foods to be served on this day are citrus fruits, herbal tea, and honey cakes. The usual activities and traditions done during Litha are making wands, leaping bonfires, charging crystals, fairy magic, and harvesting herbs.

Lammas (August 1)

The Lammas represents the first of three harvest festivals of the year. It represents the first harvests of early grains and corn. During this time, rituals of sacrifice are also common which is believed to bring in successful harvests for the rest of the year. This celebration is named after Lugh, a Celtic god related to sporting skills and the sun.

Other name for this celebration is Lughnasadh. The preferred food served during the celebration is cider, sunflower seeds, summer squash, corn, and fresh bread. The common activities and traditions done are playing games of skill outdoors, making corn husk dolls, and baking bread from scratch.

Mabon (around September 21)

This celebration falls on the day of the autumn equinox where the length of the day and night is equal, but the weather begins to grow cold as winter approaches. Mabon is considered as the second harvest festival of the year and rituals of thanksgiving abound.

Mabon is also known as cornucopia and autumn equinox. Preferred foods served on this day are anything containing blackberries and grapes. Turkey is also served. Traditions and activities done on this day are giving to the poor, making and drinking wine.

Samhain (October 31)

Samhain is also known as All Hallows and Hallowe'en. Preferred foods at this time are anything that contains apples and pumpkins. Activities and traditions celebrated at this time are carving Jack o' lanterns in pumpkins, remembering the dead, and divination.

Chapter 8: The Wiccan Altar

The Wiccan Altar does not have a specific guide or rule on what to put and what not to put in your altar. The important thing is this is a sacred space and as such, you must treat it with respect and not clutter it with too much of 'non-magical' items. Generally, you can let your personal creativity to guide you in creating your Wiccan altar, but here are the basic tools that you would want to display:

- Decorative items like plants, crystals, food, bells, and others
- Items or statues that represent the Goddess and the God
- Your Book of Shadows
- Candles
- Cauldron
- Wand
- Knife or Athame
- Pentacle
- Goblet or chalice

Altar Layout

It should be filled with tools and figures that you enjoy using to worship nature and deities as you see fit. However, there are a few methods for altar layouts that can help enhance the organization of the altar. Whether or not this is more effective than other methods is up for debate; again, you should go with your instincts and do what you feel is right.

Top Right (North East): God symbol. This could be a golden candle, a statue of the Horned God, an antler, an acorn or anything else you'd like to use to represent the God, or a masculine deity of your choice. A pentacle and a small bowl of salt can also be placed here to display the Element of Earth.

Top Center (North): This is an ideal spot to have a censor so that the smoke can flow over the entire altar and clear the energy around the space. However, a stick of incense can also be placed on the middle left side of the altar to represent the Element of Air.

Top Left (North West): Goddess symbol. This could be a silver candle, a statue of the Triple Goddess figures, a special stone or anything that you associate with the Goddess or Goddess deities that you wish to honor.

Middle Right (East): This is a section where incense or feathers are placed to represent the Element of Air.

Middle Center (Center): A pentacle is an appropriate tool that should be placed in the middle of an altar, although it can also be placed on the top middle to represent the Element of Earth.

Middle Left (West): This spot is where a blue candle, cup, chalice or bowl of water may be placed. These can be used for blessings, drinking potions or representing the Element of Water.

Bottom Right (South East): This is generally where ritual knives are placed, including an athame and boline. Wands may also be placed here.

Bottom Center (South): The bottom center of your altar is where you would generally keep your spell materials, such as a specific type of candle, a piece of paper or crystals that you're currently working with. There should also be a red candle in this space to represent the Element of Fire.

Bottom Left (South West): A chalice or cauldron can be placed here depending on how much room you have.

Some people have square-shaped altars (as opposed to the circle-shape described above) with each corner having an Elemental candle, a Spirit candle on the top and a pentacle in the center. An altar doesn't have to conform to any layout and you can design it as you wish. Some people even have more than one altar, including one for magical work and another specific to deity worship. The choice is yours for however you wish to practice.

How to Build a Wiccan Altar?

An altar is defined as a central point of personal worship where you identify most with the surrounding energies as well as the invocation of the gods. Ideally, an altar should be a place where you can find peace and inspiration, and the Wicca use it to conduct basically any ceremonies that pertain to their belief. For that reason, spells, incantations, and even the gifting of offerings is done therein. Building an altar is imperative among the Wiccan and in the case that you are interested in casting spells. There are a few steps that are included in the building of altars; these are detailed below:

Decide where to place the altar

Altars are not limited to a particular location, and you can place them either within or outside of a building. Some witches have their own natural altars constructed at their premises, while others have portable ones which can be transported from location to location. Most people prefer to have the altars either in their backyards, which are open to the moon and nature, or in their bedrooms, due to privacy issues. The bedroom is also quite relaxing, and many people find that they are able to meditate effectively there.

What to make the altar out of

There are usually a lot of themes that determine what an altar is supposed to be made out of. Depending on the location of the altar, you can choose to have it made out of metal, wood, plastic, or basically any other material that is easily accessible to you. Wood is usually a popular choice due to its ability to be found easily, as well as the fact that it can be polished and designed to create a very attractive finished product. Some people go out of their way to use exotic materials such as glass and marble, which affirms that it is all a matter of preference and the value that one places on the altar.

What to put on it?

This is often the most complex part of the process, and it involves determining the symbols and tools that will be placed on the altar. As has been discussed, the different tools and symbols are used for invoking different gods and energies; hence, it is important to consider what exactly it is that you are trying to achieve. Some of the tools and items that you can place on the altar include bowls with salt, candles, bells, a wand, an athame sword, incense, and basically any other object that you'd like to place on it. You must add a personal element, such as your picture or one of your belongings, so as to create a union of energy.

Chapter 9: Principles of Wicca

In order to begin to truly understand what Wicca is and what it means to be a Wiccan, you should first learn about the following basic principles of Wicca:

- We have a responsibility to live in harmony with nature by caring for Mother Nature and ensuring that there is an ecological balance. This works within an evolutionary concept that offers the fulfillment of life and consciousness.

- We live in acknowledgment that there exists a power that is greater than that which is known to the average person. We recognize the "supernatural" because it is super and greater to be naturally available to all people.

- The Creative Power reveals itself through the masculine and feminine aspect present in all people. This Creative Power reveals itself when there is an interaction between the feminine and masculine. The two are complementary to each other and none holds more power or importance over the other. Sex is valued as an embodiment of life, as pleasurable, a symbol of life and an energy source that is used in rituals, worship, and magic.

- Both the inner and outer worlds are all spiritual and their interactions are the elements that are used in magic. Both are valued at the same level with equal reverence.

- We honor those individuals who have invested their time and energy in leadership and those who share their found wisdom and insight. We do not worship an authoritarian hierarchy.

- How one sees magic, wisdom and religion are determined by their lived experiences in the world. The philosophy of life is recognized as Witchcraft in the Wiccan way.

- A person who seeks to use the energies used in nature' processes to guide their own reality in the physical realm is a "witch." They do so to live in oneness with the universe, to gain wisdom while revering the Earth and living beings.

- We affirm that life is the progression of evolution recognizing the development of consciousness whilst providing meaning to the universe as well as living our purpose in it.

- We are opposed to other philosophies of life and religions that attune themselves as "the only way" while suppressing other practices and denying others to fully explore insights available in the universe.

- We are only engulfed by our present and future and we do not care about the illegitimate claims of the craft and its history.

- We do not believe in the individual gain sought from the suppression of another nor do we gain power from other people's suffering. We do not recognize the "devil" and the concept of absolute evil.

- Within nature, we seek that which is essential in the development and contribution of our wellbeing and health.

Reverence for Nature

The word "pagan" has many different meanings. For the definition of Wicca, pagan refers to someone who practices and believes in spiritual, religious or community nature worship. Again, the word "nature" can also have many meanings. In this case, nature is all life forms (biologically and geologically) that make up the natural world. This usually excludes civilization and human activities, but NOT humans themselves. Humans are a part of nature, not separate from it.

Many Wiccans and pagans feel a kinship with trees, animals and rocks. The idea is that we are all connected on a scientific, physical level as well as a spiritual, divine level. Just as the earth's ecosystems connect biological and geological forms and features together, there is also a spiritual or magical force that unites all of us, making us timelessly equal and intertwined. Based on this concept arises a great respect and love of nature. Wiccans may celebrate and honor nature by some of the following actions and ideas:

- Respecting all life forms and refraining from maliciously harming others, from flowers to insects to forests. Some practice nature worship by being vegan or vegetarian while others simply live sustainably and ecologically conscience (for example, using all parts of animals for food and practicing eco-friendly farming). The way you honor nature is up to you, as long as you remain respectful and take the time to understand the natural cycles of the earth.

- Volunteer or donate to local parks and wildlife centers. These are places that work to protect animals and preserve their natural habitats. By volunteering, you'll be putting in your physical and spiritual energy toward a cause that directly benefits nature.

- Plant a bee garden. Bees, including honey bees and bumblebees, provide incredibly important ecosystem services. They help pollinate a large percentage of the food that we eat, so giving back to them by planting a bee garden is a great way to honor nature and the services of bees.

- Practice sustainable living, including recycling and using less resources. By doing more for the environment, you can show your gratitude to the earth and help to preserve its resources for future generations.

- Walk or bike instead of drive. Even the smallest difference in carbon emissions from your car can contribute to lowering global emissions. While it may not feel like you're making much of a difference, there's plenty of other benefits to walking or biking (for one, you get to be closer to nature!).

- Take time to learn. Spend time with nature and allow yourself to truly understand it. Read a book about your local wildlife or natural areas and discover what there is to know about the world around you. By simply being more knowledgeable about nature, it's possible to make more informed choices about how to become a wise advocate for animals and the environment.

Mother Earth and The Elements

One of the biggest principles in Wicca is the reverence and worship of the Earth Mother. She is our home and all of her creatures, herbs, trees, forests, people, and elements are a powerful magic that requires respect through the ritual of Wicca. In order to work with the beliefs of Wicca, you must accept that nature is the divine power within us all and there is no greater power other than what lies beyond Earth's surface.

There are Pagans and Wiccans who worship very specific plants and herbs in relationship to what their religious purposes are; however, many Wiccans will support a wide variety of magical ritual devoted to the Earth and her bounty. In order to express the accurate sentiment about how Wiccans work with nature, here is an example of an exercise that you can do to fully connect with the wisdom and magic of the wild kingdom:

Go into a forest where no one else can see you. Take off your shoes and feel the Earth with your bare feet. Lie face down on the forest floor. Rub dirt on your cheeks. Smell the moss and the mushrooms. Plant wet kisses on the bark of trees. Hold hands with the shrubs and the plants that you see and listen for what they will say to you. Ask for guidance from the forest to show you which way to walk. Let yourself be governed by the land and see where it takes you.

It isn't just a love of nature that is a belief of Wicca; it is the full and powerful relationship with it so that you are living in harmony with it and its rhythms, cycles, expressions, and energies. Many of the spells and rituals you do will involve a reverence for nature as you call upon the elements to invoke your magic practice.

The elements are one of the most authoritative aspects of the Wiccan circle. Working with the following four elements is the bread and butter of Wicca and a key factor in how you practice your spells and cast: Earth, Air, Fire, Water. Using these elements is a powerful incantation to directly pull nature into your magic circle. It is the honoring of the great forces of nature that have the power to give life and take it away.

These four elements are wonderful ways to get started exploring the basic principles of nature; they are divine and without them, we would not live. Worship of these elements is a major facet of Wicca and developing your connection and relationship to them is a must with Wiccan ritual.

Bringing the Principles into Daily Spell Work

All of these principles will come together to help you work with Wicca and the spell work and rituals that come from the belief in these principles. Knowing what you will want to bring into your daily spells and rituals will come from the guidance you receive from nature and the world around you.

The elements will always play a part in your basic spells. Every time you cast a circle of protection; you will include the 4 basic elements. Deciding what type of daily ritual or spell you want to perform may be directly related to the phase of the moon or the season of the year you are in. It could also be that it is a particular god or goddess that you are invoking to work with their energy in your growth and your life and that you need certain elements of that nature to create your daily spells.

Whatever way you are working with Wicca, the principles and beliefs are the foundation of the magical work you will do on your journey ahead. Knowing and loving these aspects will help guide you with your practice and give you the grounding you need to be a fully open Wiccan, celebrating the cycles of life through the magic of nature, the elements, the moon, and the gods and goddesses of the great divine spirit.

Chapter 10: Deities & The Divine

At the core of Wiccan belief, there is a fundamental idea that within and among the world (and the universe), divine energy exists. The definition of these figures varies among individuals, but they are essentially two dualistic figures who can manifest themselves in one or many forms. The Goddess and the God can also be interpreted as symbols for various aspects of the world. They are part of everything; not above us, but within us and around us.

The God and the Goddess may be seen as equal but opposite entities or figures, often representing masculine and feminine energies. While they are traditionally seen as male and female, that doesn't necessarily mean that they are sex or gender exclusive; it simply means that they are two parts of the same whole with opposite energies.

The relationship between the God and Goddess is usually that of divine lovers. They can be seen as the mother and father of life, as well as the dually opposite energies that exist in everyone and everything. The most important thing to remember is that they are completely equal; one does not rule over the other and both work together harmoniously.

In traditional beliefs, The God and the Goddess are NOT a situation of "good versus evil". Wicca ties in with the cycles of nature, and nature is far from black and white. There are aspects of both dark and light within the Goddess and the God, just as each of us have a darker and lighter side. Neither is better or worse than the other; both sides have different meanings and messages to learn from. This goes for the idea of life and death as well. In Wicca, death is not seen as something terrible and final. With death comes life and rebirth, just as leaves fall and grow again during the cycles of the seasons.

Honoring the Deities

There are several different ways you can honor and worship Wiccan deities depending on your personal choices and methods of practice. Many Wiccans simply regard the God and Goddess as dualistic forms of divine energy that lives all around us, and that's about it. The God and Goddess can have different ways, including showing of gods from various cultures. When casting spells Wiccan would call upon that specific god depending on the type of spell they are casting.

Wiccan don't bend down when worshipping instead they embrace the divine because it is around them. The deities are called upon to help in making decisions, guidance and advice.

The Goddess

Names like mother earth, moon goddess and triple goddess are used for the goddess.

Mother

She is termed to be a symbol of fertility, sexuality, power and the giver of life. She is seen as the full moon; ripe and swollen with stability and magical energy. She is called upon when casting fertility spells or spells for inner strength and fulfilment.

She reminds wiccans to enjoy life by healing the wounds and strengthening their spirit She is always there to whisper about fears and pain we face. She is mighty in strength yet calm in nature. Some examples of the mother goddess include: Durga, Hestia, Frigg, Buffalo Calf Woman. Corn Mother, Hera, Isis, and Demeter.

Maiden

The young maiden goddess represents virginity, birth, new beginnings, youthfulness, and growth. The Maiden is shown in the waxing moon, which is the growing phase of the moon as it moves from new to full. The Maiden is the representation of growing change and starting new avenues in life, such as finally pursuing your dream job or growing your family. The maiden can bring about joy, but she can also be fierce, naïve and innocent. There is a warrior-like spirit to the Maiden, and we can see that in hunter-goddesses such as Artemis. There is also the spark of the creator, and goddess who rule creativity and divine inspiration, such as Brigid, are represented by the Maiden.

The Maiden is pure potential. She is just beginning, and so blesses all apprentices, students, new love, new endeavors. She is the writer before a blank page; the painter before a new canvas, and the farmer surveying an un-tilled field at the earliest sign of Spring.

Some of the many goddesses who embody the aspect of the Maiden are: Artemis (also known as Diana), Aphrodite, Amaterasu, Brigid, Freya, Kuan Yin, Persephone, and Oshun.

Crone

The crone is the wise, mature form of the Goddess who carries a deep understanding of life and death. Her essence can be found in the waning moon when endings occur and lessons are learned. Like death, the Crone form of the Goddess should not be feared. She is there to guide you through the toughest of times and help you learn from your mistakes so you can put an end to things and move on. The Ancient Greek Goddess Hecate is frequently tied to the Crone; she is the goddess of herbology, magic and ghosts. The Crone is the Triple Goddess in the aspect of wise elder. She is deeply magical, full of wisdom and secrets. She retains the curiosity and inquisitiveness of the Maiden, the loving nature of the Mother, but as Crone, has gained mastery over the magical arts. She teaches us that the end of life is simply the pause before the circle continues: death precedes rebirth, and so the Wheel continues.

The Crone is as mighty as the other aspects, but in her own way. She uses knowledge to enhance Her power. When she teaches, her lessons may be more stern than the other faces of the Triple Goddess, but they are just as loving. The Crone guards the secrets of prophecy; this is two-fold. She has seen all that life can give and so can easily predict the future based on the information presented to her in the present; she also knows the ancient divining ways, and is happy to gift these to younger generations.

The Crone keeps to Herself in her studies, and so to connect with Her, you need to go calling for Her. Like Baba Yaga in her chicken-legged hut in the forest, the Crone sits and waits, absorbed in the magic of the universe, until the grandchildren come knocking for treats and lessons.

Some of the many goddesses who embody the aspect of the Crone are: Baba Yaga, Badb, Ceridwen, Elli, Hecate, Kali, Lara, Macha, The Morrigan, Nepthys, and Oya.

The God

While the Goddess may seem more frequently discussed in many groups, the God is an equally important figure in Wicca.

Horned God

He is the ruler of the wilderness and the symbol of virility, hunting and wild animals. His horns or antlers have nothing to do with the Christian figure of Satan; instead, they are actually symbols of his masculinity, sexuality and association with wild nature. In some Wiccan beliefs he is also aligned with death (in opposition to the Goddess, who is life). This doesn't mean he's evil, because death is not evil. He is frequently represented by the Celtic god Cernunnos, an antlered deity of animals, wealth, fertility and the afterlife. God is both the Hunter and the Keeper of the forest. He is united with the Mother goddess in symbolic fertility rites to celebrate the abundance of the land and the fields. Many consider Him to be the male equivalent of the Triple Goddess, as He rules over birth, life, and death as well as the afterlife.

Some of the many gods who embody the aspect of the Horned God are: Herne the Hunter, Janus, Pan, Osiris, Dionysus, and the Green Man.

The Green Man

The Green Man, also known as Herne, originated in Britain and is connected with the woodlands and the fields. He is a shepherd of beasts, keeping a watchful eye on the animals of the wilderness. The Green Man is often depicted as having a wild, unkempt crown and beard of vines and leaves. You can still see images of Him in ancient churches throughout the United Kingdom today. The Green Man and the following Horned God are often viewed as the same deity.

Sun God

The Sun God is born from the Mother Goddess during winter (still too young but growing as the days get longer). During the springtime, he has matured into a young man who has begun courting with the Maiden Goddess, symbolizing the growth and fertility that comes with spring and the onset of new life. During the summer, the Goddess and the Sun God are wed and the God begins to mature to his peak strength when the days are at their longest. During the fall, the Sun God begins to grow tired and the days grow shorter. In the meantime, the Goddess is pregnant with the Sun God and ready to give birth during the winter, continuing the cycle all over again. The God worshipped in his role of the Sun is observed throughout the Wiccan Wheel of the Year. At Yule in December he is reborn, and so we are given hope during the shortest day and the longest night that soon, there will be less darkness in the world. At Beltane, the Sun has just reached adulthood, and His youthful spirit and enthusiasm is evident in the raucous, rowdy Maypole dances and bonfires. At Midsummer, the Sun has reached His pinnacle of power, and we bask in his loving rays until Harvest comes at Lammas, where He lays his own body down into the fields to give us the very last nourishment of the year.

Some of the many gods who embody the aspect of the Sun God are: Apollo, Balder, Freyr, Garuda, Helios, Lugh, Ra, and Surya.

Oak King and Holly King

He takes hold of the throne in the winter and the Oak King reclaims his rule in the summer, with their battles taking place at Midwinter and Midsummer. The cycle continues eternally as the two bring balance to one another, a symbol of how the seasons cycle across the earth in a continuous process of birth, death and rebirth. **The Oak King** represents the brighter, warmer half of the Wheel of the Year, when we are nearer the sun and its life-giving rays. The Oak King is born at Yule, grows in strength during the rest of Winter and early Spring, then becomes a virile young man at Beltane, finally to assume the height of His power, seated at the Midsummer throne during Litha. By the time Harvest comes at Lammas, He is in decline. By Samhain, the Oak King has passed.

The Oak King represents warmth, passion, direct action, and confidence. He is physicality and prowess, the steady arrow shot from the hunter's bow. He represents male virility and the power of creation.

The Holly King represents the darker six months of the Wheel of the Year. He is born during the bonfires of Midsummer, and ascends the throne as His counterpart rescinds it. The Holly King rises to power during the darkening days and hours of the harvest, of Samhain when the veil between the worlds is the thinnest, coming to His full potential soon after. At Yuletide He rules with all of His power for one brief night, then passes on as the Sun begins to make its way back from the darkness.

The Holly King represents subtly and the wisdom of the trickster. He is cold and logical, physically sly as the fox, a keen blade wielded in the dark. He represents wisdom, secrets and the power of the storyteller.

Deciding Whether Or Not to Incorporate a Deity Into Your Faith

It is up to the Wiccan as to whether they decide to reach out and connect with a deity or deities as part of their spiritual path. It is not required. Many find that they need to work out feelings about authority figures or parental roles before they can begin to forge a relationship with an otherworldly being.

Some things to consider when deciding this is that, unlike Judeo-Christian or Abrahamic faiths, Wicca does not hold that we are *subservient* to the God and Goddess—also referred to as the Lord and Lady. We are their children, and loved by Them. Sometimes we may have our own issues to work out regarding our mothers and fathers. That is normal and natural. Some Wiccans prefer to view the gods as teachers, masters to our apprentice role, wise and patient, ready and willing to hear about our fears and misgivings.

Still others turn to the gods as peers and friends. None of this is disrespectful. Intention is everything, and if you choose to approach and reach out to a god or goddess, know that your intention and your heart will be read by Them fairly and with reciprocated love. We honor Them by speaking to Them; we contribute to the pulse of Their spirit with our own. While not ever deity teaches lessons the same way—some may be playful and fun, others healing and infinitely patient, still others may be quiet and stern—they all have ancient wisdom to share, and they are happy to share it.

If you decide to walk the path of nature alone, and prefer not to connect with a god or goddess, that is completely acceptable. Some Wiccans devote a section of their altar to their ancestors and beloved dead. And some merely seek to connect with nature.

Chapter 11: The Wicca Elements

The five Elements may be perceived in a variety of ways because each element has a different meaning for different people. However, there are several general correspondences that many agree upon when it comes to the symbols and meanings behind each of the five Elements. When it comes to your personal practice, choose tools and figures that you feel belong to each element. When you follow your heart and instincts, you will enhance your inner power and ultimately strengthen your relationship with the Elements.

Earth

Earth is the solid foundation of our lives. It's the strength that holds us together and grounds us in times of chaos or stress. Earth is the rich soil under our feet, the beginnings of growth and the ultimate recycle of life into death as our bodies return to the ground. Earth can be representative of abundance and prosperity, relating to the wealth of life that can be grown from a bountiful harvest.

The colors associated with the Element of earth are green (grass, plants and trees), brown (soil and wood), yellow (leaves and sand) and black (stone and rock). Ritual items and tools associated with earth include rock crystals, stones, salt, gems and cords. Earth figures and animals include species associated with dry land and forests, such as wolves, bears, horses and bovines. Earth is usually tied with the North direction, the Goddess and feminine energies.

In rituals, you can call upon the Element of Earth for spells that require prosperity, grounding, fertility and luck with money or employment. To invoke Earth during ritual, bury items outside in the earth, plant flowers or draw images in soil or sand with a stick, wand or your finger.

How to Practice Earth Magic?

Stones and rocks: Although different types of stones and rocks can be associated with specific Elements (aside from Earth), working with them is a great way to get in tune with Earth's power. Try using stones, rocks, gems and crystals in your magic work, prayer or simply as a charm or talisman that you take with you. Try choosing a stone or crystal that really resonates with you and makes you feel grounded, secure or even lucky. Choose a method to bless it or charge it with magical energies. You can do this by gently and safely passing it over the smoke from a candle or incense. You could also leave it under moonlight overnight; letting crystals and stones soak in a full moon's light overnight can give it a powerful charge for enhanced magical properties. If none of that feels right, simply take the stone in your hand and meditate or think positive thoughts until you feel the stone emanate comforting warmth in your hand.

How do you choose what stones and rocks to use? Your decision is totally based on your feelings; just pick something that has personal meaning for you or draws you in. Examining rocks at a nearby river or stream is another engaging and natural way commune with the earth and spend time out in nature. Always make sure to follow local laws regarding rock collection (you may need to have a permit to take them home). It's best to enjoy and leave them out in nature where they're supposed to be; the earth will thank you for it and your spells will be that much more powerful! To shop for safe and affordable stones and crystals, check out your local new age shop and find something that calls to you.

Drums and cords: Sacred drums and personalized cords are a few tools you can use to embrace the Earth Element during meditation or magical practice. Listening to the deep, rich rhythm of a handmade drum or tying sacred knots with cords in different colors and patterns is not only emotionally therapeutic, but also spiritually satisfying. Imagine the pounding of the drum as the slow, powerful beat of the earth and picture the cord as the earth's binding strength that unites us all.

Gardening: If you feel a strong connection with the Element of Earth, one of the best ways you can practice and celebrate Earth magic is by gardening. There's nothing that feels more earthly than digging your fingers into dirt, planting the roots of flowers and growing your own vegetables straight from the soil you worked with your own hands. Even if you have no outdoor space for gardening, you can still buy indoor herb gardens and house plants to tend to (make sure to choose pet-friendly versions if you have animals in your household). In return for your love and care, plants will provide you with cleaner air and nutritious or aesthetic value.

Air

Air is the refreshing breeze that flows across our skin and makes us feel more alive. It's the energy and knowledge that we accumulate throughout our lives as we sharpen our minds through study and experiences. Air is the wisdom and intelligence passed down between generations that sparks our creativity and connects us all together. Air can also be associated with psychic powers, wishes and telepathy.

The colors for Air are yellow (brightness), pale blue (clear sky) and sometimes gray (clouds). Feathers, fans, incense and wands are all magical tools frequently associated with air. Musical instruments, such as flutes or harps, can also be used to involve the Element of Air as they symbolize intellect and energy. Animal figures connected with Air are avian species such as eagles and songbirds or insects such as dragonflies or bumblebees. Air is usually more closely related to the God, masculine energies and the East direction.

Calling upon Air during magic work is great for spells that involve divination, the desire for freedom, academic success or safety while traveling. To perform a ritual associated with air, you can gently toss objects in the air, use a fan or feather to wave through the air or try calming breathing exercises.

How to Practice Air Magic?

Musical instruments. When playing a wind instrument, you are using physical air as well as embracing the Element of Air by producing fresh, auditory tunes. Even if you're not very good at any instruments, just practicing with a few notes is enough to engage with Air and get your spiritual juices flowing.

Feathers and wands. Using feathers and wands in Element magic or rituals is a great way to call in the Element of Air. Keep in mind that you should not pick up feathers out in the wild as there are several laws restricting the take of feathers that could belong to endangered bird species. Instead, use feathers from domesticated bird species without restrictions, such as chickens, geese and turkeys (always refer to your local laws for specifics). Keeping at least one feather on your altar is a beautiful way to honor Air. You can also use the feather to cleanse the space and fan incense smoke during rituals. Similarly, wands are another Air-inspired addition to your altar. Wands can also be used as magical projectors or amplifiers in any kind of magical work.

Traveling. Visiting wide open spaces, such as rolling, grassing fields or open beaches, is a great way to appreciate the Element of Air and get a dose of freshness. These places can be very cleansing for the spirit. If you stand against the breeze, imagine it rushing through you and carrying away all of your negative energy and dark thoughts. Allow it to cleanse you and relieve you of unnecessary emotional weight.

Fire

Fire is the emotion we feel when we fall in love or protect our loved ones. It's the driving force behind our choices and our willingness to get up and keep moving forward, despite our hardships. Fire is the pain we experience but ultimately benefit from as it helps to make us grow. The Element of Fire is aligned with sexuality, cleansing, destruction and inspiration.

Fire colors are red and orange (flames and lava). Objects related to fire are items related to warmth, hotness or sharpness, including candles, spices, swords and athames. Many Fire animal figures are lions or reptiles such as the snake as these types of animals are often associated with warmer environments. Fire is tied with the God, the South direction and masculinity. The Element of Fire can be invoked for spells that involve protection, sex, strength (both physical and emotional) or the banishment of negative thoughts and energies. For fire rituals, you can use both controlled indoor (candles and cauldrons) our outdoor (campfire) flames and smoke to burn, smolder or heat objects for spells.

How to Practice Fire Magic?

Candles, incense and cauldrons. The use of fire-related tools is quite common in many rituals, regardless of if they're surrounding the Element of Fire. Fire is a very powerful tool because it can burn away items, produce smoke and leave ashes behind; all of these things can be used for a variety of spells, such as love or blessing spells. For indoor witchcraft, lighting candles and burning pieces of paper inside a fireproof cauldron or cup is generally a safe way to perform Fire Element spells in a controlled setting. Always remember to use caution when working with flames and make sure not to leave burning candles in a house unattended. Some spells require that the candle burn itself out while you do other things; just be sure to keep an eye on it and keep it away from other objects that it could set on fire.

Outdoor fires are especially powerful for any type of ritual, particularly when performed under the light of a full moon. Bonfires are frequently held for different Wiccan festivals and days of celebrations. This is because the symbolism of burning wood outside under the sky is often quite powerful when it comes to celebrating the Elements as well as the Goddess and God. Again, always make sure to be careful when working with fire and always keep fire in an open space with a water source nearby. For outdoor Fire Element rituals, many Wiccans will dance, sing or chant as they circle around a bonfire or campfire. Others will simply gaze into the flames and perform visualization magic or meditation.

Spices and cooking. If you can't use actual fire, you can still use tools and objects to represent the Element of Fire. Spices, such as cinnamon and allspice can be placed in a small pouch or mixed in ceremonial beverages to represent Fire. Using witchcraft in cooking and baking to bless or ritualize different foods is also a fun and engaging way to celebrate the Element of Fire while dually helping to sustain yourself or prepare for Wiccan holidays. Rather than using sweet or creamy sauces, season your food with peppers and other spices to bring forth the spiritual energies of Fire.

Water

Water is the rejuvenation of your spirit when you thought all was lost. It's the hope you feel when you look into the horizon and experience emotions rise in your chest and fill your whole body. Water is seen in the healing of wounds, both physical and emotional. It can also be reflected in birth and motherhood. Water is an Element of emotions, purification, sleep, dreams and friendship.

Ritual colors for water are varying shades of blue, mainly dark blue (oceans and rivers). On an altar, Water-related items can be cups, chalices, seashells and any other objects that are able to hold liquid or relate to bodies of water. Animals connected to the Element of Water are primarily fish and marine mammals such as whales and dugongs. Water is frequently represented with the Goddess, the West direction and feminine energies.

How to Practice Water Magic?

Chalices and bowls. Chalices, cups, goblets, bowls and cauldrons are all tools that can symbolize the Element of Water, regardless of if they're filled with liquid or not. Filling these items with blessed water is a great way of purifying the altar space. There are several different ways that altar water can be blessed. One way is to hold the cup or bowl in front of you and invoke the Goddess while visualizing the water in the bowl as being purified. Another powerful way to bless water is to leave it out under the light of a full moon and allow it to soak up the moon's energies overnight. If you can gather it naturally, salt water from the sea is an incredibly potent liquid for casting spells related to Water or performing purification rituals.

Potions, brews and other concoctions. Heatproof bowls can also be used for making sacred or magical brews for potions or ceremonial drinks. For example, drinking a love potion can strengthen a spell related to relationships and romance. Potions can be made from a mixture of natural ingredients, such as wine or juice, and used in rituals to become very spiritually powerful infusions. Brews are usually thicker and may even contain food items for consumption or enchantment. Witches bottles can also be filled with liquids, herbs and other items to be used for protection spells as it acts as a vessel to absorb unpleasant energies. Always remember to use natural, non-toxic ingredients when making potions and other concoctions.

Bathing and swimming. Running a sacred bath is a great method for immersing in the Element of Water and preparing for rituals by cleansing your body and figuratively washing away negative energies. The Element of Water can be an excellent source of healing, especially when accessed in wild spaces. If possible, swimming in a clear, natural lake, river or ocean can be a very powerful and sacred experience that every Wiccan should consider. Take some time to soak up the natural, wild essence of the Water

Element and allow your spirit to be filled to the brim with peace and positivity. Let the waters rush over your skin and carry away any pain or fear you may be keeping locked up.

Spirit

Spirit, sometimes also called Aether, can be difficult to describe as it comes in many forms and exists in all things. Spirit is connection you experience when you walk through the forest or feel a kinship with wild animals. It's the joy you feel when your loved ones are close to you in a positive situation. It's the combination of all the elements and the eternal cycle of life and death along with reincarnation.

The color for spirit is usually white, but it could also be black or combination of various colors appropriate for each spell. The Element of Spirit doesn't have any specific animals associated with it because it can be seen in any species; some use the dove or a white stag to represent spirit in certain situations as these animals are generally a sign of peace or purity. The direction and gender for Spirit is universal and androgynous (a combination of masculine and feminine characteristics).

Spirit can be acknowledged on an altar with a white candle, but the majority of the Spirit Element will lie within yourself. Breathing softly and clearing your thoughts is one way to engage with the Element of Spirit.

How to Practice Spirit Magic?

Spiritual meditation and lucid dreaming. Meditation is frequently utilized by Wiccans and non-Wiccans alike because it's an effective exercise for detaching from chaotic thoughts and stress. To meditate, you'll need a comfortable and quiet place where you won't be bothered. You can sit or lay in any position that's fairly comfortable for you (you don't want to get so comfortable that you'll fall asleep unless you're trying to do lucid dreaming). Once you've settled in, you should start to slowly inhale and exhale. Try focusing completely on your breathing.

Visualize negative energy being exhaled from your body and positive energy being inhaled. If you find yourself getting distracted, you can try saying a mantra to help you focus. At this point, you can begin to visualize yourself in places out in nature, such as a large forest. This should be a place where you can completely relax and be yourself. You may also encounter your own manifestations, such as an animal guide or spiritual manifestations of the divine.

Chapter 12: Understanding Wicca Rituals

Put simply, a ritual is a specific series of behaviors and practices that are enacted sequentially for social, religious, spiritual, emotional or ceremonial purposes. Rituals are commonly associated with landmark moments – births, deaths, marriages – and they can bring joy, ease sorrow, or just celebrate something major. Rituals are in essence repetitive – like a routine. The same order is observed every time the ritual is performed, and many people find security in that familiarity.

Witchcraft rituals also follow this basic pattern, and many date back thousands of years. The only dogma attached to witchcraft is the exhortation to 'Harm None,' so the pagan ritual immediately becomes something meaningful, since it is not based around doctrine. Pagan rituals demand that you pause and take stock of what you are doing and what you hope to achieve through the ritual. It is designed to focus your intent on whatever the ritual is intended to accomplish.

One thing pagans believe is that rituals are best conducted outdoors, to enhance the connection with Nature, and emphasize the sacred bond between the Earth and its people. They do not need buildings made by man in which to conduct their rituals, preferring outdoor spaces such as caves, cliff tops, hillsides, woods – even private gardens. The connection with the Goddess is more perfectly achieved outdoors.

So effectively, a pagan ritual can be conducted anywhere – they do not need a consecrated building, because they cleanse the area where the ritual will be performed, before marking out the sacred circle. So 'where' is not particularly important, but 'why' is crucial. As has already been noted, witchcraft is about knowledge – the word 'witch' derives from a word meaning 'wise.' So the first thing you need to know is why a particular ritual is performed, before you move on to the 'how.'

Many pagan rituals are centered around the seasons, and particularly the moon's phases, which is why timing is often important. For example, whether a ritual is performed with the waxing or waning of the moon can significantly change the purpose and the hoped for outcome. Another thing to remember is that witchcraft rituals are designed and intended to focus on the positives in life, rather than the negatives. Rituals are a way to remind yourself of your hopes and dreams, and attract positive energy and positive people into your own sacred circle. Witchcraft rituals remind you of the sheer scope and size of the Universe, and the powers of Nature that can be harnessed through rituals designed to celebrate life and Nature in all its glory.

Essentially, the major difference between pagan rituals and, for example, Catholic rituals is in the way people participate. In a Catholic Mass, the priest leads the ritual, and the congregation responds at the appropriate times and in the appropriate manner. It can all become rather automatic, and maybe even meaningless for some people. It's something they do out of long practiced habit.

In witchcraft rituals, there are no leaders and followers – all are equal, and all have a part to play in the ritual. While the elements of the ritual are very important – the sequence of events, the tools used, the words spoken – the real purpose of the ritual is to connect with Nature and the Gods on a subconscious level, which is where witches believe true connection can be felt. The reason for conducting the elements of the ritual in the same order every time is not to indoctrinate, but to allow the mechanics of the ritual to eventually come as second nature. That means the mind can be freed from the task of thinking what comes next and concentrate on what the witch wants to bring to and take from the ritual.

A typical ritual will begin with preparation, including the definition of purpose, writing appropriate words, assembling the tools needed and preparing the area to be used for the ritual, as well as the body. All rituals begin with the casting of the circle - the endless, sacred space in which all are equal and safe from harm. Then the Quarters are called. This is acknowledgement and welcome for the four main compass points and the elements of Fire, Water, Earth and Air.

The next step is to invoke the Gods and connect with them, before stating the purpose of the ritual. Then and only then can the rite, itself, commence. This is when the mental energies of the participants are focused on the purpose of the ritual, and it is during this phase that what witches call 'true magic' occurs. The rite is followed by a period of meditation, before the Gods are thanked and the circle is closed. The first ritual that a new member of a coven will experience is an initiation ceremony. The ceremony is also called "Rites of Passage". Traditional Pagans may choose to work sky clad, while modern Wiccan and neo-pagan practices call for the use of ritual robes. The robes' color can be seen as just as impactful as the use of color in other magical tools. White robes are commonly worn during the initiation ritual and anytime the members of the coven may need extra protection. Ritual robes are believed to enhance the wearer's sense of mystery and magical energy. Donning the ritual robe is considered a mental and spiritual experience that helps the wearer connect with what they are about to do. Most Wiccans do not wear anything underneath their ritual robes. Robes can be pretty much any color or pattern and can be as long as the heart desires. Make sure to not use excessively long robes during rituals and spell work involving candle magic. Other practitioners choose to only wear a cloak, although they can also be worn over the ritual robes. The design of the outfit is completely up to the ritual performer and can include hoods, sleeves, sashes and other modifications. Most solitary practitioners just choose to wear an outfit that is special or in some way has meaning to them, rather than donning the traditional ritual robes.

In accompaniment with special clothing, Wiccans wear at least one piece of magically charged jewelry during the ritual process. Both women and men regularly wear crystal necklaces, anklets, rings and bracelets. Some Wiccans will even wear delicately crafted jewel or crystal encrusted headpieces. Necklaces will often be worn in addition to the crystals that depict Wiccan symbols, such as the pentacle. These pieces are worn to enhance the wearer's personal energy and ability to manifest more energy into their reality. The practitioner decides the importance of this aspect of rituals, but many people find it helpful to "get in the zone". Any ritual or spell requires a great amount of manifested energy in order to effect changes. To properly contain this manifested energy and keep any negative forces away from you, a magic circle must be cast.

A magic circle is very similar to the psi ball. It is an energy field that you visualize around yourself or a sacred space, which serves two different purposes in witchcraft. The first is protection from external dark energies. The circle must be cast with the intention that only good energy may exist within it, or you will leave yourself vulnerable. The circle is usually six feet in diameter. Its second purpose is to enclose you and your energy inside of it. It can be represented in the physical world by drawing or carving out where the visualized circle would be and placing candles with elemental symbols at its four cardinal points. These points are North, East, South and West. If candles are being used to outline the entire circle, use four larger candles at each cardinal point. To ensure the full power from each direction and its relation to the physical elements use a symbolic representation at each point. Crystals, rocks, plants, or ceramics can be used to represent North/Earth. Feathers, incense or sage bundles work great to represent East/Air. Candles are the main item used to represent South, because its corresponding element is Fire. Finally use seashells or a chalice of water, to represent West/Water. As well as using physical symbols of the elements, the candles placed at the cardinal points may also be colored coded. This can be thought of as a direct connection to the five elements represented in the Pentagram.

The Earth is the element that represents the Goddess, so it is customary to honor her first before honoring any other element. Traditions or rituals that focus on ancestral worship, on the other hand, begin in the West. This is because the west is commonly associated with the underworld as Water, its symbolic element is seen as the method of passage into deaths realm. Different traditions have different ideas on how the "Calling of the Quarters" ritual should be performed. These range from being strict and annually ceremonial in traditional coven settings to a particular way being the most comfortable for the solitary practitioner. The methods of Quarter calling include symbolic gestures, incantations either spoken or meditated on, or by the use of four different musical instruments, each symbolizing an aspect of the direction it is calling. Once the quarter has been called, an often-colored candle is lit and placed on its coordinating cardinal point. The strength of the flame of each burning candle signifies the strength of the connection to each direction. Once all four candles are in place within the circle, you are free to start any witchcraft practices needed to ensure your desired outcome of the future.

Magic circles can be cast and recalled using a magic wand. Wands are used as a divination tool to channel magical energy and are commonly made of a natural material, such as wood. Different types of wood can be used to symbolize something meaningful, or used in rituals that call for specific plants. When not using a magic wand, it should be placed in the south quadrant of your altar, to charge its power over will and transformation. Before closing the circle, the act of "Dismissing the Quarters" should be performed to dismiss the directional energy. This ritual releases all that was called upon and ultimately harnessed during the "Calling of the Quarters". Without performing this act, it can make rituals feel incomplete. Many feel it impedes on the balance of magic and therefore, the symbolic balance of the universe. To dismiss the Quarters, the same ritual used to call them should be done in reverse order. This process is known as moving "widdershins" around the casted circle. Widdershins means counterclockwise, or against the sun. This process is only done at the end of ritual acts and it is considered bad luck to perform rituals this way as well. The term for clockwise is "deosil", which translates to the opposite of its partner and means sun-wise, or with the sun. The process of dismissing the Quarters is subjective, personal to the performer and dependent on the method used to call the Quarters in the first place. As the quarters are released, the candles placed in the four designated spots should be snuffed, unless any of them were lit at the evocation.

The Correct Way to Perform Rituals

First of all, note the title chapter. It could have been 'The Right Way to Perform Rituals,' but that would suggest a type of blueprint – do this, do that, don't do this and never, ever do that. The point here is that there are many, many different ways to perform rituals, depending on the personal preferences of the participants, the purpose of the ritual, the location, and numerous other factors.

It's no exaggeration to say there are probably millions of permutations for performing witchcraft rituals. However, there is a sequence of events that needs to be observed if you are to obtain everything you require from your rituals, and this is what is meant when referring to the 'correct' way. If you haven't already noticed, witchcraft is both a personal and a universal religion, and when it comes to rituals, the personal is very much to the forefront.

Preparation

The word 'ritual' does not suggest spontaneity. A ritual consists of certain elements, performed in a particular sequence. Whenever the ritual is repeated, the elements and sequence will also be repeated. Witchcraft rituals are also like that – they are designed with a purpose, and in order to make the ritual work as you want it to, you need to prepare thoroughly. That means preparing yourself, the items you will use during the ritual, the area where it will be conducted, and the words that will be spoken during.

You may wish to consider what – if any – clothing you will wear for a particular ritual. Does it require a ritual bath, or just normal bodily cleansing, which should be part of the ritual preparation anyway? All these things need to be considered during the preparation for the ritual.

This preparation serves several purposes, and it is important to the success of the ritual. Preparation concentrates the mind on what will take place during the ritual, and what you are seeking to gain from it. And if your preparations are thorough, you can relax and enjoy the ritual, because it is something to be enjoyed, rather than endured.

Tools

While the word 'tools' might smack of the mundane, it's the word many witches use to describe the items they use during the performance of rituals and the casting of spells. This is an area which is open to individual preference and practice, because while there are certain tools that form part of all rituals – such as the broom, wand, candle, chalice, cakes and ale (or wine, water, cider, fruit juice or tea – see what is meant by individual choice?).

Then there's the Book of Shadows, which is more practical than it sounds, and not at all menacing. It's basically a workbook for witches, where everything to do with rituals, spells and the practice of the Craft is recorded. It's a highly personal book, and at one time it would have been hand written. These days it's likely to be a loose leaf binder full of word processed or photocopies of spells, rituals, preparations, recipes – in fact, the Book of Shadows contains the life of the witch, if not in a nutshell, at least in a folder. It makes sense to use a loose leaf binder, then you can move the pages around to make it easier to conduct the particular spell or ritual you happen to be involved with.

Other items you will use during a ritual are representations of the Goddess and the God. These will be the deities you identify most closely with, and your choice will influence the characteristics of the rite, because deities, like people, are all different. There will also be representations of the elements – more about these in casting the circle. A bell or bells will also be used at various points in the ritual, usually to signal a progression, or a new stage. And a pentagram is integral to the ritual, and to everything you do as a witch.

If you like to use music during the meditation phase of the ritual, you'll need headphones and a source of music. A smart phone with the sound turned off so your ritual cannot be interrupted by a phone call is a good option here. Finally, don't forget a lighter or matches for the candle. It's usual to place all these tools on a ritual altar. Now everything is ready, you can go ahead and cast the circle for the start of the ritual.

Casting the Circle

This is probably the most important part of any witchcraft ritual. The sacred, never-ending circle, where all are safe and equal, is very significant in pagan practice, so this is one part of the ritual that has to be right. Before beginning, the area of the circle will be ceremoniously cleansed with the broom.

Then the Elements will be invited to the circle with the invocation to 'Be present and watch over the circle.' Wording for this is very much a personal choice, as is the method of invitation for each element. The Element of Spirit, and possibly Guardians, Angels and Spirit Guides, depending on the purpose of the ritual, will then be invited, and finally the Goddess and the God. The sacred circle is a protected place between worlds, where negative energy and powers are excluded.

Now it's time to align with the Goddess and the God (always ladies first), state the purpose of the ritual, and then visualize it through meditation, as if it is already happening. The ritual could be a simple thanksgiving, or a statement of purpose for motivation for a new beginning, or pretty much anything, but to this point the ritual will follow the same course. The words used in the ritual will define the purpose, and should come from the heart, even if they have been prepared beforehand. Now you will drink half the wine (or whatever is in the chalice) and eat the cake. The rest of the drink is usually returned to Nature by tipping it into the ground after the ritual.

Then it's time to thank everyone for being present, close the circle by going in the opposite direction to the one used for casting, using the wand and visualizing the closing. Finally, the witch or witches will tidy up after the ritual. Casting a circle of protection is a basic yet vital skill that every Wiccan should learn before engaging in magic. Remember that each time you perform magic or conduct a ritual, you risk attracting malignant forces. The purpose of casting a circle is to create a high-energy zone around you that will drive off negative beings that usually vibrate at a low frequency.

- The first step would be to select a suitable environment. Spell casting and circle casting can be done indoors or outdoors. However, spells tend to be stronger with the latter because of the direct connection with the natural elements. Whichever you choose, make sure that it is somewhere you won't be distracted, preferably someplace that's free from human technology.

- While some Wiccans choose not to mark out their circle of protection, beginners are advised to do so. You may arrange candles or crystals at the cardinal directions (North, East, South, West) or at the pentacle's points. Use the Wiccan tools to represent the spirits of the earth (Earth, Fire, Wind, Water).

- The next step is to invoke the divine powers of the universe to enter the circle. For this, you may pray to your God or

Goddess. The deity that you will call upon sometimes depends on the nature of the spell or ritual. For instance, when casting a love spell, naturally, it is appropriate to call upon the Goddess of Love.

- Position yourself at the center of the circle. Every part of your body should be inside the circle.

- Envision the divine power as a liquid silver-white light being poured into your crown, filling the vessel which is your head.

- Extend your arms, palms facing out, as if to embrace the divine power. Each time you breathe in, more of the blessed liquid light flows into your head. Each time you breathe out, the light radiates from your palms. Continue this visualization until you are able to spin a protective cocoon of light all around your body. At this point, your entire being is vibrating at high frequency. When this happens, you become capable of attracting positive things, persons, events, and experiences which vibrate at a similarly high frequency.

- Next, extend your right hand toward the circle's edge. Spin yourself three times following a clockwise direction. Visualize yourself spreading the powerful light in a circular pattern.

- Then, with two arms lifted to the sky, call upon your God/Goddess to bless your circle.

- After this, you may begin to cast your spell or perform your ritual.

- When you're done making your spell, you are expected to close the circle of protection. This is done by extending both arms. Spin yourself in an anti-clockwise direction for three times. See the divine light scattering and evaporating, and exiting the circle.

- Finally, thank your God/Goddess for blessing your circle with their divine presence.

Chapter 13: Wicca Symbols

Symbols are considered to be some of the most powerful things that human beings have ever created. Though symbols are just drawings, the meaning derived from them is immense. Wicca uses symbols as signs and as parts of magic. Some symbols are regarded as elements while others are representations of very deep ideologies. Some of the basic symbols used by the Wicca are as follows:

Pentagram/ Pentacle

In modern times, the pentagram is a highly controversial symbol that most people associate with devil worship. As illustrated, the pentagram consists of a five-pointed star which is within a circle. According to the Wiccan members, the five-pointed star is an illustration of the aspect of key energy-giving and protection properties. The star is a representation of the five key Wiccan elements - air, water, fire, earth, and spirit. The fact that the elements are enclosed together is considered to be an illustration of all aspects of the world coming together, representing one divine. The fact that all sides of the triangle are pointed can be thought of as an illustration of the victory of spirit over typical matter. Today, the pentacle used by Wiccans can be equated to the star of David in Judaism.

Witch's Knot

Wiccans use the knot by scratching it on their doors in order to protect themselves from evil spirits and all negative spells that may have been cast against them. The witch's knot has the ability to be drawn into a continuous motion, which increases its efficacy. The Wicca magicians also use this symbol to bind some things magically. Whenever the symbol is drawn, there is always a sense of peace, as any negativity is bound and cannot enter.

The Triple Moon

The triple moon is considered to be an illustration of feminine power, and it is used in the Wicca traditions to represent the goddess. The three moons are symbolic of the three phases of the moon: waxing, full, and waning. As a mother, the aspect of fertility, fulfillment, and nurturing capabilities is achieved, since a mother typically cares for her little ones. The final stage is crone, where the female is a bit elderly and has acquired a considerable amount of wisdom and knowledge in the course of her life. Death and rebirth is part of this final phase, which makes it a rather bittersweet eventuality. In Wicca, the triple moon is largely an invitation for the women to begin celebrating each area of their lives.

The Horned God

Just like the triple moon, the horned god has three major phases which include the Father, Master, and Sage. However, unlike the triple moon, which is more inclined toward females, the horned god is considered to be more correlated to males and is actually thought of as encompassing the male aspect of divinity. Usually, the word "horned" leads one to think of the term horny, which is essentially where the males are known to get their virility.

This symbol is another major source of controversy in current times due to its association with the element of devil worship, although the truth is that there is no correlation.

The Ankh

The Ankh is considered to be one of the most powerful Wicca symbols, and it is mainly associated with healing. The symbol is drawn on entrances of either the houses of Wicca members or in their places of meeting, and it particularly comes in handy whenever there is the invocation of spells pertaining to healing. The Wiccans refer to the symbol as the key of life, since it is associated with the union between the god and goddesses, which therefore prompts the creation of infinite power in the universe. The top and circular loop usually represent the feminine energy, while the vertical bar facing down is a representation of the male energy.

The Elven Star

The Wicca associate the symbol with the seven directions, with the original four being east, west, north, and south, and an additional three directions, including above, below, and within. In addition to the direction, some of the priests and priestesses view the symbol as an illustration of the faery path, which includes reputations such as connection, trust, magic, joy, honor, inspiration, and knowledge.

The Wheel of the Year

The wheel of the year denotes the eight seasons of the year, also known as the Sabbats. With the wheel, the Wicca are able to navigate through the ever-changing seasons with ease, just like a wheel moves and rotates easily from one point to the other. The wheel is divided into the eight Sabbats, and it is considered to serve as a reminder to the people that they should get moving, as nothing is constant.

Incorporating the Wiccan Symbols

Since you now have full knowledge about some of the most common Wicca symbols, it is worth knowing how it can be incorporated into the personal space of a member, as well as what exactly the Wiccans are supposed to use them for. There is no limitation as to where the Wiccan can incorporate the symbols, and they can paint them and place them all around the house, carve them into jewelry, or hand paint them on the walls. Every Wiccan member is free to display the symbols however they wish; at the end of the day, the ability to follow all of the regulations is what matters.

Chapter 14: Preparing For Spell Casting

Shielding is done prior to spell casting to envelop yourself in a protective layer. Otherwise, you will become vulnerable to negative energies.

Grounding, on the other hand, is all about merging your energy with that of the Earth's. You can either draw from the earth's energy to replenish your own reserves or you can release your unwanted, energy into the earth. The former is useful at times when your productivity is low. The former is useful when you're suffering from stress, anxiety, anger, or grief. When you ground yourself before spell casting, you are borrowing energy from the earth so that you won't end up depleting your own energy resources. You may also perform grounding to clear your mind and ensure that your intentions are pure before making a spell. To get started, you will need to find a quiet place and get comfortable. Meditation can be done almost anywhere, but you will need to feel relaxed while you practice. This means that sitting or kneeling will often be best as there will be less of a strain on your limbs. To begin with, all you will need to do is relax.

Close your eyes and listen to your breathing. Rather than focusing on all of the external events that are happening around you, take a moment to attend only on the movement of air as it enters and leaves your body. Breathe in through your nose and out through your mouth. Do not try to hold your breath for a specific amount of time, simply find a comfortable rhythm and settle into the process of breathing in and out, noticing how the air moves through your body.

Once your breathing is familiar, begin to relax your body. Feel the weight leaving your legs, your arms, your chest, and eventually your head. Still focusing on the breathing, be sure to not let any outside thoughts drift in. If this happens, don't panic or worry. Simply remember your breathing and realign yourself. Hold this for however long you are comfortable.

After a while, you will notice a period of levity and lightness. A sense of warmth and peace washes over the practitioner. The stresses, worries, and noises of modern life begin to ebb away, and you are left with just your breath as it moves in through the nose and out through the mouth. After enough time has passed, slowly ease yourself out of the state.

For those who spend more and more time meditating, the rewards begin to become more and more apparent. As well as being relaxing, it can help you reflect on personal problems and the problems of others, shutting out all of the clamor of everyday life and allowing you to focus on what really matters. While it might not seem like a traditional witches spell, this self-reflection is a key aspect of the occult.

Once you have mastered the art of mediation, then you will be able to move on to the next practices that we will be using during the spell casting. One of these involves the setting up of candles in certain ways. At various times throughout the guide, you will be asked to lay out your candles along what is known as the cardinal points. Put simply, this means placing one candle on each of the compass points, forming a cross or a square as you do so.

This will mean that you have one candle on each of north, south, east, and west. Some spells will then require these candles to be lit in a certain order, but that will be specified in the particular spell. Once you have laid out the candles in the correct manner, then you will be able to proceed with the spell.

Another practice that might seem strange or unfamiliar to those who have not practiced the art before is the idea of centering yourself. To center oneself is to realign the mind to focus on the task at hand. Not dissimilar to meditation and very alike the modern practice of mindfulness, it will involve the expulsion of irrelevant and unconnected thoughts and being able to devote yourself to the spell which you are trying to conduct.

This can be easier to accomplish than meditation. To complete the process, it can help to have a distinct object or item which you wish to focus on and which you wish would occupy your thoughts. At the expense of everything else, you should focus on this. If you feel other thoughts encroaching on your mind, then simply let them drift away, freeing them back up and into the ether. Rather than purging your mind, it is more a case of allowing the thoughts to dissolve into nothingness, allowing you to be free to focus on the task at hand.

Grounding (Receiving Energy)

- Find a comfortable position. You may sit or stand as long as your spine remains erect.

- Inhale and exhale deeply for a few times.

- Close your eyes.

- In your mind's eye, see yourself turning into a tree. Your arms are ligneous limbs. Your feet (if you're standing) are sprouting roots. These roots are digging deeper and deeper into the earth, taking hold, clinging to its life source.

- Then, imagine the energy of the earth as a liquid light traversing the tunnels of your roots. That infinite power is being absorbed by your roots, being absorbed by your being.

- Now envision that light moving up your spine. Feel the loving warmth running up your back, towards the nape of your neck, and up to the top of your head. As it does, imagine that light filling every vital part of your body-your stomach, your heart, your neck, your face, your brain. See that light fortifying each single thread of your being until you are positively glowing with the love of the earth.

- Continue doing this until you feel completely energized.

Grounding (Releasing Energy)

- Assume either a sitting or a supine lying position. Your arms should be at your sides and the palms of your hands must be flat on the ground. The goal is for your body to be in full contact with the earth.

- Close your eyes. Perform deep breathing.

- Concentrate on pinpointing where the negative energy within you lies (ex. your chest)

- In your mind's eye, see that negative energy as dark liquid. Now, envision that energy moving inside your body, going down towards the direction of the earth, almost as if the earth is siphoning it from you.

- Visualize all that dark liquid moving from your heart, down towards your arms, towards your palms, and finally, being absorbed by the earth.

- With each ounce of liquid leaving your body, feel yourself becoming lighter and lighter, freed from your burdens.

- Imagine the earth drinking up every last drop of this vile liquid until your entire body is purged.

- Shielding

- The first step is to invoke happy memories and to think about the things that you are grateful for now.

- Each time a happy thought emerges, hold onto it. Caress and cradle it in your mind.

- In your mind's eye, see each happy image as a brick. Use these bricks to build a wall around you.

- Imagine each memory, each reason to be grateful, piling up on top of the other.

- Keep doing this until you are able to envelop yourself in a fortress of happy thoughts. Be sure that you are protected on all sides, from bottom to top.

There are Wiccan practitioners who have tried shielding themselves with negative thoughts and memories instead of positive ones. The price to pay is that other individuals who are in tune with the universal power can sense these energies. When this occurs, they can intrude your thoughts and memories. They will increase these negative energies and direct them back to you. In the end, you are likely to feel disgusted with yourself.

Chapter 15: Instructions For Spell casting

A spell refers to a magical formulation that is normally intended to trigger a magic effect on either a person or an object. The spells are normally created through the chanting of a series of words, singing, or even mere speaking. The series of words are known to have magical powers, and a person or object under a particular spell have their actions and thoughts dictated by the specification of said spell. Usually, the spells are cast by witches or groups of persons who believe in their powers, and they are believed to cause instantaneous reactions.

Creating your own Wiccan spells is actually simpler than believed to be. While most witches and spell casters usually use ancient spells created by other people, there are times when they want to use customized and specific spells. In this case, the writing of individual spells is imminent.

It all depends on your preference, if you want to perform spells or not either way, it is not compulsory to do spells and magic in order to be Wiccan. Further, if you want to create or do spells, remember the crede "Harm None" as this is an essential part of Wicca. It doesn't mean that if you perform spells, you can destroy your enemies this is NOT true! If this is your motive for becoming a Wicca, then I suggest you stop reading this book as it won't get you near your goal. So, I repeat, the practice of Wicca is to commune with nature and to open the realm of the gods and goddesses to be one with them through connecting with nature.

The Steps

When it comes to witch craft, making a spell is easy it's just like creating a new home cooked meal recipe; but, of course it requires practice. So, let's just stick to how spells are generally done and later on I will give you some of my tried and tested spells for love, money, and healing.

Your Purpose

The first step in doing a spell is to know what the purpose of the spell is. The goal has to be specific. For example, if you are looking for love, a love spell won't do the trick because are you already eyeing someone? Or maybe you want an ex to come back to you? Or maybe you still need to meet that special someone. This is how specific your purpose should be.

Materials

The next step if finding the 'perfect' spell and gathering all the necessary materials to do the spell. You can also make your spell by making use of 'correspondences' as these are lists of items with their corresponding purposes. Take for example you can use the herb Damiana which corresponds to lust and love. To make a spell, would need around 2 to 5 items are sufficient. You can also make use of crystals or candles and work with colors too.

Words

When casting a spell, using words best help you to focus your intention and energy. There are also spells that already have words included. But if you are making your own spell, then you have to be creative when it comes to creating chants.

Timing

Although this is not as important as other steps in casting a spell, but with right timing it can add additional power to your spell. For a little magical boost, you can pick the right phase of the moon or the right day of the week. Check out some correspondence tables to boost the power of your spell.

Put It All Together

Many people believe that just by chanting the words of a spell and going through the motions will lead to a successful spell. But in reality, what makes a good spell powerful and successful depends on your focus. You have to focus on what you are doing and you have to take your time. Thus, it means you need to learn the spell before you begin. You also need to visualize the energy and your intentions as vividly as you can and this is the hardest part when casting spells because it takes practice and experience.

How to Create Your Own Wiccan Spells following the aforementioned instructions

The following represents a simple formula to create your own spells:

Identification of the key intent/goal of the spell

Before you get down to the writing of a spell, it is vital that you begin by establishing the key intent/end goal. Each and every spell works to achieve a particular purpose, and you must be able to identify exactly what you want to achieve. People cast spells for different purposes. These purposes can include the desire to find love, success, employment, or good health. Through the creation of the spell, the major goal is attracting exactly what you want to have in your life. Whatever the main aim is, make sure to attain specificity. Examples of intentional aims include the following:

- I will get the advertised job.
- I will be promoted to the next level.
- I will find my soul mate.
- I will heal from arthritis.

In some instances, you may want to write a spell that is directed to another person. It may be that you would like good fortune for the other party or you would like to punish them for something. Whatever your aim is, you must keep in mind that karma is real and that what you cast upon others can come back to you at any time. It is for this reason that one of the basic tenets of Wicca practice is the stipulation that you must take care that your activities do not bring harm to others.

Determining and assembling the materials needed

In the course of casting a spell, there are various materials that are required for specific spells. You must determine what materials you need to use in order to be successful in the casting of your spells. According to Wicca, the greater magic often lies in the symbols, which makes it imperative to learn some of the basics symbols that pertain to your spell and use them. Notably, the fact that the Wicca tradition is ancient does not mean that the use of current items is out of bounds. The wheels of cars, sunglasses, and even chess boards can be used as long as you are clear about what they are meant to symbolize.

In determining the materials, you will use, you must always keep in mind that spells serve two key purposes: to either attract something into your life or banish something. The former is usually positive while the latter serves as a protection against aspects such as illnesses and spells cast by other people. The materials used to achieve the two are very different, hence the need for clarity. Currently, there are very many books and publications that help you choose the materials and ingredients; it is ideal that you decide upon those that most appeal to you.

Decide on the timing

As has been stated, most of the spells are very time-specific, although there are a few that are not. In most cases, the timing of the spells is highly dependent on the phases of the moon, as some spells are cast during the full moon and others are cast in alternate moon iterations. In most cases, spells that are supposed to bring positivity and beneficial inferences to you are conducted during the full moon or when the waxing moon appears. Destruction spells or generally negative spells that are required to banish some of the retrogressive aspects from your life are conducted during the waning phase. In as much as the specific details are really not as important as they seem, it is worth understanding that the energies during the particular phases are different, which makes it imperative to ensure that you follow the periods as much as you possibly can. It's worth noting that you can write your own Book of Shadows based on your individual experiences when casting spells, and the greatest aspect that you must observe is to be immensely confident about what you are doing.

Figure out the words

For spells to work, specific incantations and chants must be used. As the Wiccan say, there is power in words. There are no words that are chanted in the spell making that are void. Therefore, you must be very clear about what you want to say before you actually get into the casting phase. Currently, anyone can have access to the hundreds of Wiccan spells that are found both online and in publications, and you can identify the specific one that you wish to use. Some spells are meant to call the gods for assistance while other spells are used in poetic inferences. However, all work the same, and the only thing you need to do is make sure that by making the chants, you will invoke the particular occurrence that you desire.

Setting Up Your Altar

An Altar is a space of devotion to something. It can be anything you want it to be and creating your altar is the artistic expression of your magic and your practice. We all need a place in our homes that reflects our most important desires and passions as well as our thoughts and expectations. An altar is a perfect way to create a physical manifestation of your spiritual journey.

There are no rules to setting up your altar and often times, it will change with you as you grow and evolve. It takes on the life you are living as you add and subtract things from it based on the intentions and practices you are doing.

Altars are a reflection of who you are and what you are praying to and so while you develop your own altar, be clear about how it shows off what you are choosing to align with at all times. It needs to be a place that has a flow and an energy of harmony and balance. It may be necessary for you to tend to your altar daily or frequently to maintain its energy and ability to attract abundance into your life.

Your altar should be in a place in your home where it cannot be disturbed easily by others and can be easily seen by you so that you are always alive to it. Many people put altars where anyone can see them and that is perfectly okay; it doesn't need to be hidden; it only needs space to exist undisturbed by anyone but you.

The altar of your choice can be on a bookshelf, in a cabinet, on top of your dresser, hanging on the wall, *etc.* It is up to you to choose the right place for your altar to exist. Once you have found the proper location, you can acquire the items you need to create it and decorate it.

Often times, people will use a cloth to lay out on the surface of wherever it will sit. It could be something small, like a scarf or a handkerchief or it could be something more meaningful, like a piece of heirloom lace from your Grandmother. You don't have to use a cloth at all, but if you choose to, make sure it is something that reflects the overall energy of your altar.

Next, you can start bringing in objects to help you align with your spiritual path and purpose. Many people place sculptures or figurines of their favored gods and goddesses, others may use paintings, pictures, or photographs to set out as an homage to a particular deity. Anything goes really and it all depends on what you like and what you are wanting to focus on.

Another approach is to just use the items from your tool kit. You can place these items on the altar and dedicate this space to your sacred rituals so that your tools are always resting on your altar. Essentially, building an altar for your magical tools. Bringing focus to these items through the display on an altar will remind you of the importance of working with this magic and will help you continue to honor your Wiccan practice. When you are opening your energies to work with your tools, you can start by lighting candles on your altar, burning some incense or smudging the altar and starting your rituals in this way.

Your altar is basically a display of your internal magical self. It is a reflection of your power and your curiosity to ask questions about the great unknown and to worship the energy of all things in this world. Bring to your altar anything that is resonating with you at the time. You may decide to decorate it with fresh cut flowers and let them wilt and dry to illustrate the idea of life and death.

You may also want to collect items from your nature walks to devote the altar to Mother Earth. It can also be a place that changes with every Wiccan holiday celebration making your altar a devotion to the seasons and rhythms of the Earth.

Don't be afraid to alter your altar. It can transform with you as you grow and it will need to be tended to the way you tend to yourself. Treat it like a living thing and as an expression of yourself. Whatever water you keep on your altar, if any, needs to be clean and pure; don't let it get dirty and stagnant as that will be a sign showing you that you are neglecting your altar and your spiritual practice.

Tend to it and allow it to be a consistently transforming part of your life that invokes a deeper spiritual reflection of your journey.

Asking the Gods/Goddesses for Support

Whether you are looking for guidance from the gods and goddesses of Pagan ritual or not, letting yourself be open to their assistance and guidance is a good way to bond with the energies of all things as you work with your Wiccan practices. You may not have a particular deity that you work with or devote your altar to but as you are preparing your rituals, it is a good idea to let the universal energies know that you are ready to tap in and find help if it is offered as you cast your spells and perform your rituals.

All you have to do is say the following words as you light the candles on your altar and burn your incense:

"I am opening the lights of all life to the energy of all things. I ask for guidance, support, and protection from the Great Mother and Father and all offerings from the spirits and deities of all life. I am open to receive your love, light, and warmth as I progress in my ritual. So mote it be."

You can change the wording to be anything that feels right for you based on what energies you want to call in to help. You may be more inclined to practice fairy magic or to work with the animal kingdom of spirit guides. You may also desire to connect with your ancestors as you begin your rituals and spell castings. All of these ways of connecting to that work will help you, so make sure it is in alignment with how your individual Wiccan practice is for you.

Change the wording of the above message to reflect your practice but keep the message the same. Stating that you are open to receive help and guidance is a very powerful tool of connection. Maintaining a desire to only work with the energies of light and love is an important factor because it declares that you are wanting to work with the higher vibrations and that you don't want to call on anything harmful or low energy like a trickster spirit or energy who may not be as helpful as other energies will be.

Opening yourself to all of this will help you concentrate even better on what your intentions are and what you are wanting to accomplish with your spells. Relax, ask for support, and give thanks to all the energies that come to provide you with help along your path.

Casting Your Circle

You don't have to use your altarpiece to cast your circle. You may be out in the woods when you need to cast and will be far away from your altar. It might be also that you just utilize your altar to store your magical tools between casting and won't need to involve it in your Wicca work; however, you may find that you feel more grounded in your practices if you start by connecting with the energy of your altar before casting your circle. It is really up to you how you choose to work with your own energy and magical tools.

Why do you cast a circle and what does it even mean? When you are invoking the energies all around you and connect your own energy to the spiritual plane, you need to have an opening and closing of intention and protection. It is a helpful way for you to have clarity and focus while you are performing rituals and casting spells but it also serves as an intentional centering of your energy and attachment to your spiritual self. Casting is almost like a meditation to get you engaged with your work.

The meaning of casting a circle in your preparation is also to align you with the four directions and the four elements. Each way you travel is represented by your circle and each element of the life spark is represented to connect you to your full purpose and potential. It is a meaningful acknowledgment of your journey when you cast a circle and it brings into focus that which helps you succeed on your path: the directions and the elements.

Spells, Rituals, Intentions

The next step in the process of a typical spell or ritual is the actual spell work or ritual work that aligns you with your intentions. Remember: it is important to have clear intentions before going in, so before you cast your circle, ask yourself: what is my magical purpose today?

Once you have clarity about what you are wanting to achieve or focus on, you may want to design your ritual or spell from your own personal idea of how it should go or you can use already existing spells and craft work that feel natural and good for what you are wanting to accomplish. There are tons of spells online, in books, all over, that can help you choose the best way for you to align with your craft work.

Much of what you will be doing in this step is clearly detailing and stating your intentions to create the energy of life around it. It may include herbs and other items that support your intention. If you are celebrating a holiday or a specific god or goddess, you will be working with those items and energies specifically to enhance your ritual or spell.

Words are important and you may need to write down ahead of time the words you want to share once you have opened a circle. Preparing for your ritual or spell is just as important as executing it. Prior to opening your circle, write down the words for your spell on a piece of paper. Gather the herbs you wish to include in your circle, or the relics and objects that will be meaningful to you.

There are so many unique possibilities for how you can invoke your own powerful magic and let it be known to the energies of all that surrounds you. The following steps are simple ideas and clues for how you can get started with creating your ritual and spell. Remember that practicing Wicca is a creative and artistic experience and there really isn't a wrong way to do it. You can use the following steps to help get you started with building a spell and/or ritual.

Set your intention. Write it on paper, on leaves, on stones or pieces of wood to burn, on anything magical. Gather your ingredients. You may be working with herbal remedies that support your intention. Make a bouquet of them to dry on your altar. Collect the stones, crystals and any other earth elements that feel appropriate and place them where they feel best. You may want to collect sacred water from a waterfall or a river that feels magical to you. After casting your circle of protection and power, you can now begin your ritual with your objects and intentions. Using your written intentions as a declaration is a wonderful way to open yourself up to the energy of what you are wanting to accomplish. Don't just write it on the paper or the leaves; read it aloud so that you can feel the words come out of your mouth with sound and release the words into your circle.

Closing Your Circle

Closing your circle is as simple as opening it. All you have to do is pay respect and gratitude to the elements and to the directions. You may want to face each direction again to ask the directions to comfort you on your path as you allow your spell to take effect.

You can also connect with the elements you have in your space and carefully return them to their altar space as a way of creating closure with them. Here are a few steps to help you close your circle, as you opened it:

Thank each element by addressing it directly. Example: Thank you to the earth that grounds me (sprinkle salt or soil into your hands and rub them together, letting the salt/soil fall away natural). Thank you to the air that blows me forward on my journey (snuff out the smudge stick). Thank you to the fire the lights my way (blow out candle). Thank you to the water that cleanses and purifies (dip fingers in water and flick on your altar or on your own face). Stand up or point your energy in the direction of each of the four directions to thank them for their presence, similar to the way you did it with the elements in Step 1. All you have to do is offer gratitude and move through each direction, closing the circle the way it started.

Alternative: You can combine Steps 1 and 2 and close the circle by thanking each direction and the corresponding element simultaneously.

A final thank you can be expressed to the Great Mother and the Father or whichever gods/goddesses you have invoked for your ritual.

Casting spells requires a lot of confidence and belief that whatever you are invoking will come to pass. You must not have any doubt in your mind or heart, as this may hinder the full connection with the energies and the gods. Notably, casting spells using your own words and chants is considered to be more effective than using other people's spells. Whenever you use your own spell and words, the energy connection is much greater than the use of other people's creativity. Personal spells create your own signature and a unique energy connection; you just need to have total belief.

Accepting Your True Power

Wicca is a beautiful, fun and magical way to connect with your true power and the energy of all life around you. It has a way of asking you to be present and to identify your whole being and the nature of what you are seeking with a mindful appreciation of nature and all of her energies.

One of the most profound lessons of Wicca and other Pagan practices is that it is a way for you to creatively explore yourself and your inner power as you transform and grow. The best way for you to approach rituals and casting spells is to trust your own inner knowing about how the spell should go and what ways it can unfold.

You will find a wide range of variations for one specific intention or spell, because there isn't a wrong way to cast. As long as you are upholding the Wiccan Rede, then anything goes, essentially. As you continue to work with your own spell work and rituals, remember to honor your power above all else. Devotions to the Earth Mother and all of the other gods and goddesses are equally important to the devotion of your own magical powers and truths.

Chapter 16: Casting Spells For The Days Of The Week

Each day of the week is associated with a specific planet. The days of the week are also associated with specific colors, deities, and elements. While it is true that you are free to cast a spell anytime and any day you want, you can have a higher chance of being successful with it if you cast it on the right day.

- Sunday (Sun) – this day is correspond with health, happiness, accomplishment, strength, abundance, and general success.

- Monday (Moon) – this day corresponds to fertility, female energy, dreams, psychic skills, spirituality, kids, and family.

- Tuesday (Mars) – this day corresponds to dealing with conflict, conquering obstacles, independence, action, and energy.

- Wednesday (Mercury) – this day corresponds with education, career, jobs, knowledge, communication, and creativity.

- Thursday (Jupiter) – this day corresponds to legal matters, business, finances, and wealth.

- Friday (Venus) – this day corresponds with sexuality, social status, marriage, family, relationships, romance, and love.

- Saturday (Saturn) – this day corresponds with meditation, binding, banishing, overcoming habits, discipline, and protection.

Casting Spells on Sundays

Sunday is the ideal day to cast truth spells. These spells are done to help you seek for answers. They are ideal to be done if you want to get answers from people regarding something they did or said. You can cast a truth spell to find out the things that certain people refuse to tell you. Likewise, you can cast a truth spell to find out the truth behind lies. For your truth spell, you can use a variety of ingredients and tools, depending on what the spell calls for.

The following is an example of a truth spell:

- This spell requires the use of a white candle, a blue candle, a needle, five senses oil, and compelling out.

- To cast the spell, you have to use the needle to carve the name of the person from whom you want to get an answer from. When you are done carving his or her name, you have to use the five senses oil to coat the white candle. Then, you have to use the compelling oil to coat the blue candle. When you are done with that step, you have to light the two candles and place them on a table. See to it that the two candles are a few inches apart.

- You have to focus your attention and energy on the blue candle while you recite the chant you created to find out the truth and get your answer. You can use any words that rhyme or whatever has a significant meaning for you. Then, you have to focus your attention and energy on the white candle while you recite the name of the person from whom you want to get the answer from.

- You have to bring the candles closer to each other as you recite a spell that makes your intentions clearer. You have to use this spell to help you know the truth. Make sure that you let the candles burn. Wait for the flames of the candles to die out completely. When that is done, you can finally get the truth that you are searching for.

How about if you are speaking with a liar? If you think that the person you are talking to is lying, you can cast a truth spell to find out the truth.

Here is an example of a truth spell that you can use for this purpose:

- You need to prepare dried yellow roses, dried mint, nutmeg, olive oil, and a yellow candle.

- To cast a spell, you have to use the olive oil to coat the yellow candle. Then, you have to combine the yellow roses, dried mint, and nutmeg together in a container.

- When everything is ready, you have to get the candle and roll it into the mixture of herbs. As you do this process, you have to think of your desire to gain clarity and receive the truth.

Casting Spells on Mondays

Monday is the ideal day to cast spells that can help you boost your confidence level. When you cast a spell like this, you can use a variety of ingredients such as wild crystals, tree barks, wild herbs, and wild flowers. You can also use crystals such as amber, jet, azurite, and citrine. In addition, you can use wild herbs and flowers such as thyme, lavender, and bay laurel. You can also add some fragrance oils, candles, and water that has been blessed. Every element you use can help you boost your confidence as well as interact with other people much better.

Here is an example of a confidence spell you can cast on a Monday morning:

- This spell requires the use of sandalwood incense and a red candle. Sandalwood incense has an earthly scent while red candles represent strength and power. Ideally, this spell has to be done before taking a shower. Make sure that you speak slowly and loudly as you chant the spell. Refrain from whispering the words so that you can make a much greater impact.

- To cast the spell, you have to stand before a full length mirror and light the red candle. Concentrate on the flame as you work up your energy. You must feel the positive energy starting to flow throughout your body. You have to be careful not to rush the process. It may take a while before you can finally work up some energy and this is alright. When you have worked up the energy, you have to look at your reflection on the mirror. Stare into your eyes and recite the chant.

- You have to tell yourself that you are intelligent. You have to tell yourself that you can succeed in whatever you want to do. You have to tell yourself that you can speak clearly and calmly. You have to tell yourself that you can focus on the positive side of things. Moreover, you have to tell yourself that you should not allow yourself to be shaken. Tell yourself that you are intelligent and capable of achieving success one more time.

- Then, you have to visualize yourself beaming with self-confidence. Imagine yourself finally getting over self-doubts. Light your incense and let it burn as you prepare for the day ahead.

Here is another confidence spell that you can cast to serve your intentions:

- Ideally, you have to cast this confidence spell during the waxing moon or new moon. During this time, the energies that bring about confidence are high. The spell requires the use of a tiger's eye. However, if you cannot get a tiger's eye, you can simply use whatever gemstone you have. The spell also requires a yellow candle, three white candles, and a rope or wire that you can use to turn the gemstone into a necklace.

- To cast this confidence spell, you have to get out of the house and stand under the moon. You also have to arrange your white candles into a triangle position. Then, you have to put the yellow candle in the middle. As you hold the tiger's eye, you have to meditate and work up your energies. See to it that you focus all your energies into the tiger's eye. Once you feel that you have already composed yourself, you have to light the white candle and recite the chant.

- As you hold onto the tiger's eye, you have to recite the chant. By the power of three, you have to ask the energies of the universe to grant you strength and courage. Look at the flame. Focus on it. Meditate. Visualize yourself receiving the energies and imagine how you will feel when that happens. Imagine your confidence levels rising. Visualize yourself getting calmer. Take your time to envision the scenario. Allow yourself to send out the energies towards the gemstone.

- Recite the final chant, which has to be about charging your gemstone with love, light, confidence, and strength. By the power of three and the energies of the universe, you have to ask for confidence and strength to be given to you. Once you are done reciting the chant, you can turn the gemstone into a necklace and wear it. You can use the rope or wire to turn it into a necklace. However, if you are not fond of jewelry, you can keep it as a token. Feel free to charge it again whenever necessary.

Casting Spells on Tuesdays

Tuesday is the ideal day to cast spells for protection. These spells are effective in protecting you against evil and keeping you safe.

The following spell is an example of a protection spell that you can cast on a Tuesday.

- It requires the use of blue or silver glitter and a wand or staff. For your wand, you have to choose blue, silver, or white color. The spell also becomes more effective when done outdoors. However, if the circumstance does not permit you to cast the spell outdoors, you can do it inside your home.

- To do this spell, you can proceed with the steps of spell casting as usual. However, rather than begin with the North, you have to begin with the West and then move clockwise from there. You have to use your wand to tap the ground while you recite your chant. You also have to call upon to whoever guards the watchtowers of whichever direction you go to. Make sure that you ask that you may be guided through the darkness and be safe at all times.

- Once you are finished with the four corners, you have to stand in the center and recite your chant. Your chant has to be about banishing negative energies and never letting them come near you again. As you recite the last lines of your chant, you have to scatter the glitter around you and close the circle to end the ritual.

Casting Spells on Wednesdays

Wednesday is the ideal day to cast spells for better and more effective communication. So, if you are experiencing problems or difficulty with communication, you can cast a spell for it. A communication spell can help you strengthen weak lines of communication.

You can use herbs, such as chamomile to encourage understanding and improve communication. When you write down your spell, it is recommended that you use a pen with yellow ink since yellow is a color that is often associated with the element of air.

When you are ready for the spell to take effect, you can recite your chant or spell. Ideally, you should ask the powers of the air to help you send your messages to the person you want to communicate with.

Casting Spells on Thursdays

Thursday is the ideal day to cast a money spell. A spell like this can help you increase your financial stability. So, if you are experiencing financial problems or you wish to have more money, you must cast a money spell on a Thursday. However, you have to keep in mind that casting this spell still does not guarantee financial success. If you want to be a multi-millionaire, you still have to put in effort and do work.

You have to take note that casting a spell like this will only help you increase your chances of obtaining wealth. It will not actually make you rich, unless you do not make an effort to earn money. Money spells are not get rich quick schemes. They will not make you rich in an instant.

The following spell is a money spell that you can do in a few seconds. It is very simple and does not involve a lot of elements. This spell requires the use of lavender, a bag, and seven different forms of money.

You have to get the bag and put money in it. You can use whatever form of money fits you. For instance, you can put in a nickel, a penny, a dime, a quarter, a dollar, and so on, inside the bag. Then, you have to sprinkle lavender on your money and carry your bag with you for seven days.

Casting Spells on Fridays

To start casting this love spell, you have to remove the lid of the bottle of vanilla extract. Imagine that a bright red light is coming from your eyes and turning the color of the vanilla extract to red. As you visualize this, you have to recite your chant.

Your chant has to be about love. It can be about bringing love into your life, fixing a relationship, strengthening a relationship, or anything that you want to happen with regard to your love life.

When you are done with this part, you have to sprinkle a drop or two of the vanilla extract in the four corners of your bedroom. Then, you have to put back the lid on the bottle and keep it under your bed.

Casting Spells on Saturdays

Saturday is an ideal spell to cast a binding spell. Binding spells are generally used to prevent something or someone from causing harm. Unlike curses, however, they do not inflict harm on the person. They are more like protection spells, except that they aim to get rid of the negative element instead of simply wanting to be protected from it.

The following is a generic binding spell that you can cast on a Saturday. It requires the use of a cardboard, a black yarn, a cauldron, and writing tools.

First, you have to get the cardboard and write words or draw images that represent the negativity that you wish to bind onto it. Next, you have to crumple the cardboard into a ball. When you are done with that, you have to wrap it with the black yarn.

When the words or images that represent negativity are burning, you have to visualize things that represent positivity. You must feel the positive energy within you.

Chapter 17: Wicca & Magic

Magic in Wicca is the energy of nature and the Divine; it's a force that can be engaged with and even harnessed, but never fully controlled. Wiccans use magic as a tool to manifest or create changes and initiate action toward a goal. This can be as simple as casting a good luck spell or as complex as performing a spell to help you successfully change your career.

Magic is the fluid energy that flows among the physical realm but also intertwines with the spiritual world around us and within us. Simply put, Wiccans can use magic to guide change based on the choices they make.

While definitions vary depending on who you talk to, true magic in Wicca is the complete combination of personal power, nature power and Divine power. It's our inner spirit, the science of the world around us as well as the spiritual energies that connect us all. These three energies intertwine with one another and make up all that there is, making us all equal and related on a spiritual level. Most Wiccans regard science and evolution as fact; after all, nature is at the heart of science and to worship nature means acknowledging the dynamic ways that nature has evolved and continues to evolve, from the smallest microscopic organisms to the largest whales in the ocean. Many agree that even Wiccan magic works with science because dealing with magical energy is all about dealing with a combination of mental, physical and spiritual power. It's about using the strength of our minds and the forces of nature, which are fluid and ever-changing. Magic is seen every day in the world around us, because it's also tied with the wonder of nature and life itself. For example, one might experience a feeling of magic when watching the sunrise on the edge of a cliff while feeling the first rays of the sun on their face. Magic can also be in the birth of a child, the smile of a lover or the breath of a wild wolf that's never laid eyes on a human. Science is involved, of course; there's a science to the sunrise, to birth, to love and ecology. There's no reason to say that magic is absent from these things. For people who have felt it personally, magic is as natural as the rain or the ground beneath our feet.

Wiccan practice is not founded by meaningless fantasies of things that don't exist. The real essence behind Wicca is worshipping things that are more real than anything else; life forms, their behaviors and the energies that flow within them and around them. As a Wiccan, one of the absolute best things you can do for nature is take the time to truly understand it; not just acknowledging the butterflies and baby animals, but also the predators and natural disasters that occur and make up the real processes of ecosystems and environments.

Magical Record/Wiccan Book of Shadows

A magical record is essentially a witch's journal used to document experiences, magical events, ideas and any other pertinent information in their practice of magic. Some do this to document evidence or prove the effectiveness of a particular spell. It's also an excellent way to make sure the practices outlive the witch. The usefulness of a magical record, of course, depends on the how organized and how much success a witch has in his or her practices. Often times, the true value of the record isn't ascertained until it is shared with other, trustworthy witches.

The documentation typically included the mental and physical state of the witch, the time and location of the experiment, and the weather.

Magic is an illusion that is controlled and staged by magicians. This is known as the magic of illusionists. The magicians admit that the practice is a trick and that none of the occurrences are real.

Magic is created through technological devices and computerized programs, such as in the case of magical films produced by Hollywood and other organizations. This type of magic is purely fake, with most of the actions being computerized or functions of the computer programs.

In this case, Wiccan magic is extremely evident to the Wiccan people, and they are usually able to pinpoint with ease instances where magic has and has not been applied. Since magic is a normal function of their activities, they are able to feel it whenever it is in existence and utilize it in whatever way they wish. Natural magic is not considered to be a gift but rather a skill which improves as it continuously practiced.

Chapter 18: Your First Steps As A Beginner In Wicca

Now that you've been learning a little more about the Wiccan religion, you have the option of moving forward with your interest and start incorporating Wicca into your everyday life. Here are three steps to help get you started:

Learning

If you feel that Wicca may be right for you, one of the best things you can do to begin your Wiccan journey is continuing to educate yourself about the religion. Read as many books as you can from different perspectives, keeping in mind that different authors usually have conflicting methods and information. You might also consider finding a reputable advisor or open coven that would be willing to let you witness magical work or share their wisdom. Always use caution, especially when meeting people after talking to them online. Their views and individual methods of practice may be very different from what you're comfortable with, so make sure to do your research and follow your instincts.

Initiation

Once you feel that you've learned and embraced the principles of Wicca, you can have an initiation ceremony. Initiation in Wicca is a rite of passage where you are "reborn" into the Craft. Initiation doesn't have to occur in a coven; solitary practitioners can initiate themselves in a variety of ways. The ceremony doesn't have to be huge and elaborate, but it can be. In its most simplistic form, self-initiation is the process of actively dedicating yourself to the God and Goddess (or Gods and Goddesses) and the Elements.

Now it's time to incorporate Wicca into your everyday life as naturally as possible. We all lead busy lives and it may often feel like we don't have any time for spell casting, let alone having the required space or privacy. That's alright! As long as you stay dedicated to your beliefs, Wicca can be adapted for any type of lifestyle.

Practicing Wicca in Secret

Wicca is a religion based on very balanced ideals surrounding a love of nature and the enjoyment of living a fulfilled, enriched life. Unfortunately, many people have skewed or completely false perceptions of what Wicca is. Enough so that they are willing to verbally or even physically harm people who practice Wicca. If you're worried about being ridiculed or hurt by others for becoming Wiccan, there are a couple different things you can do.

If at all possible, sit down with your friends and family and explain to them what Wicca is and how you feel. Don't try to convert them; simply educate them on the general concepts and assure them that there's nothing about the religion that's evil or inappropriate. Ask them to be respectful of your beliefs, just as you are respectful of theirs.

If you're not comfortable talking to others about Wicca or doing so would put your safety at risk, that's perfectly okay. In certain circumstances for different individuals, it may be best to practice in secret until you are able to "come out of the broom closet", as it's sometimes called when a person reveals their dedication to Wicca.

In an ideal world, friends and family would accept one another no matter what religion they follow. But your safety should always come first, and you can still proudly practice Wicca even if you're unable to set up an altar or display your beliefs around others in your home. Here are a few ideas you can try practice Wicca in discretion, with or without tools:

Make a small keepsake box as your altar.

Look for a small jewelry box, chest or little storage container. You can even use a shoebox or a simple wooden box from a craft or hardware store. Make sure it's small enough to keep under your bed, in your closet or wherever you feel that it would be safe and secure. Use the box as the basis for your altar. Fill it up with sacred or personal items inspired from the Goddess, God and the Elements. These can be anything from small crystals, stones and charms to written notes, tea candles, jewelry or photographs. The most important thing is that it has meaning to you and helps you connect with magical or spiritual forces. You can get out your little altar whenever you have some time for practice, meditation or spell work. Many Wiccan spells involve lighting a candle or incense; if you can't use flame, you can use spices, unburned incense, a photo or a mental image of fire instead.

Choose a quiet, private spot somewhere outside.

If you live near a park or wooded area (provided it's safe and legal to access), look for an area where you can sit down and commune with the Divine while enjoying the splendor of nature without disturbance. You don't need to have anything with you, but you could take a journal to write down your spiritual thoughts or cast visual spells with sticks, rocks and other items you find there (just be sure to give thanks and leave them where you found them).

Keep an online blog or virtual altar.

While it may seem strange and counteractive to staying in tune with nature, blogging and using the internet for practicing Wicca is a growing method that works well for many people who are unable to practice in public or live in crowded cities where natural spaces are difficult to access. The beautiful thing about Wicca is that anyone can practice it however they want, so there's no reason why taking advantage of online practice won't work for certain people.

Many blogging websites are free and you usually have the choice to make them private or public. You can write entries as you would for a Book of Shadows. You'll also be able to post or share pictures that inspire you or help you perform visual spells. Being outside is always the most ideal when it comes to worshipping nature and the

God and Goddess, but doing what you can with what you have is better than not being able to practice your beliefs at all.

Chapter 19: Casting Different Types Of Spells

Spell for Balance and Harmony

Now it is time for some simple spells. The most important thing when casting is to have a positive mindset. If one thinks negatively, that negative energy will interfere with the spell.

For example, a simple spell to remove toxic people from your life.

- Write their full name on a slip of paper all the while wishing them luck and prosperity in a place out of your life.

- *"May (full name) find a place for them that is as wonderful and amazing as they could hope for away from my path"* (the wording isn't important the intention is) while writing, then place the slip in a glass of water and place in the freezer.

- Every day one holds the glass and repeating the chosen mantra while wishing them well. The problem is one can hold *no* animosity in themselves when doing so.

- Suppose one does the spell to get rid of a tyrant boss, and one could not get rid of their animosity completely. Unfortunately, because of the animosity it may work because the whole company moves to a different country or state, and the person is left jobless.

A lot of care must be taken with all energy transfers. One gets what they put into it. In the example above, the boss got an offer they liked but the caster's base was negative. So, while the energy put forth might still cause the spell to work to the letter, there is always blowback of some kind based on the kind of energy used.

Love Spells

- The first step is to create two letters. Using your writing tools, write a pair of letters addressed to the higher powers of your choosing. This might be a god, a goddess, or another, unspecified deity.

- Once these ideas have been committed to paper in the first letter, the second step is to create a letter detailing the ways in which you would like the relationship to proceed. Use your imagination to describe the ways in which arguments will be resolved and cracks can be filled in.

- Next, we will begin to actually cast the spell. Take the letter and move to the space in which you wish to work. With your letters in hand, light both of the candles. In this instance, the white candle will be used to represent the tranquility and peace in your life, while the pink candle will be used as a demonstration of the potential for love and affection. With both of these candles lit, move towards the flames. Take the first letter – with the criticisms and issues in the relationship and place it into the fireproof container, bowl, or dish.

A simple gambling spell

- To begin, you should be sure that you are doing your utmost to create the best possible atmosphere for the spell to work. To accomplish this, you can tailor your clothing to suit the spell. Green is the color traditionally associated with this kind of magic, so dressing in green can be very helpful. There is no need to dress entirely in a green outfit, but a small amount of clothing in the right color can be an excellent start.

- Collect your pineapple leaves and the stones you have, and place them around the area that you have created between the candles. Take the coins and space them out in front of you, placing each one with care. Finally, light all of the candles beginning with the northern point, moving clockwise, and then finishing with the central green candle (just as you arranged them).

- Light the incense, and allow the smoke and the smell to rise up and fill the surrounding space. As this happens, take the picture and consider it in great detail. As the energy begins to flow through you and the space, take the green candle and notice the wax which is beginning to dribble down the side. Drop several of these on the picture and return the candle back to the place where it was originally.

- The next step involves you taking the offering bowl, so be sure that it is nearby when you begin. You will need to place the picture into this bowl and place the bowl down inside the circle with the leaves and the coins.

Healing spells

This is a great spell for those who are trying to encourage a healing process in others. As a witch and a Wicca practitioner, you will often find that many people are interested in the kind of spiritual, energized healing that this kind of witchcraft is able to offer. Thanks to the power of magic, you can use spells such as these to help with the healing process.

- The first thing that you will need to do is to encourage your patient to relax. Just as you yourself have entered into a meditative state in the previous spells which we have covered, you can now demonstrate your learning by encouraging someone to enter into a similarly relaxed mode. Slow the breathing, and allow yourself into what is known as a "neutral mode," in which you are both relaxed.

- As you both begin to relax, you should feel the positive energies and warmth enter into the surrounding space. These might be spirits, goddesses, or whatever the various elements of your own personal brand of Wicca might involve. These are the spirits who will be helping you to heal. Encourage your patient to begin talking, expressing the various parts of their life which are positive. Whether it is relationships, their career, or anything else, encourage them to focus on the best aspects of their life, bringing these energies to the forefront.

- Remain in a positive and happy state, eliciting these emotions from the patient. Have them close their eyes, and you do the same? As well as speaking aloud, the positive aspects and energies should begin to fill the room with a warmth and a strong healing aura. Once you are happy that these spirits are present and that they are positive, you should begin to encourage them to help with the healing.

- Quietly so that your patient doesn't hear, begin to list the issues which are afflicting the patient and on which you wish the spirits to focus. During this time, the patient should be focusing on the positive aspects of their life and the things which they enjoy doing when they are at their healthiest state.

- If you have practiced the protective spells from earlier in this book, begin to create the positive shield using an aura of light. Rather than limiting this to protecting yourself, however, imagine that the light is reaching out from beyond you and layering over the patient. This healing energy will be able to not only prevent negative energies from infiltrating your patient, it will also help remove the negative aspects that might be hindering the healing process.

- Continue in this fashion. After five minutes, you and your patient should both begin to feel empowered and protected. Thanks to the layer of positivity that has descended over you both and the protective shield that has been created, the spirits that you have invoked should be able to help you with the healing process.

- Once this is complete, begin to encourage you both out of the meditative state. Talk softly and guide your patient back into the room now that they have been cleansed and protected. If needed, you can repeat this process once a day in order to bring the best kind of positive energy to your patient's life.

- As well as this healing process, the presence of nature in the patient's life is very much encouraged. It is not uncommon to find that many of those whose healing is slower than they might like have very little interaction with nature. This can be as much as adding a houseplant or two to their home or simply walking through a park. Try to suggest that they strengthen their bond with nature in as many ways as possible as this will boost the effectiveness of your own efforts.

Divination spells

While many people are aware of Wicca and how it can influence the present, few are aware of the powerful divination abilities that it can provide. Rather than allowing you to see the future exactly as it will be, the following spells will allow you to feel the energies and spirits as they move towards the future. Those who practice more and more at these arts will be able to gain a greater understanding of the shape of the world to come.

- The first step towards being able to practice the art of divination is to ensure that you have the correct tools available. For the most powerful witches, the tools are almost incidental, and the future can be seen in anything from tea leaves to dropped sticks. However, building up this level of ability is incredibly hard work, so most people begin with something a little simpler.

- A scrying mirror is something which you can make at home. It can help you to look towards the future for a better understanding of how to approach the upcoming world. While you will be unlikely to view lottery results, it can help you discern the swell of energies which surround the future. To construct a scrying mirror for yourself, you will need:

- A mirror or an equally shiny object which will provide you with a reflective surface

- Mugwort infusion (created by placing mugwort in a sealed jar with boiling water and left to stew for days)

- Because the mugwort infusion can be left to stew for so long, it can be preferable to plan this spell well in advance to be sure that you have everything available. The important part of this process is known as consecrating your mirror.

- Once you are ready to begin, fill a container with the infusion which you have created, and place the mirror flat on a table. Take a moment to center yourself, directing your thoughts and energies towards the mirror.

- At first the mirror will seem a strange and foreign object. For each witch, however, the process of learning how to use your particular scrying mirror will be unique. To get started and to discover the way in which you will work with your mirror, hang it on a wall in a room that you pass through very often.

- Close your eyes and focus your energy. When you open them again, you should be able to notice the ways in which your image alters slightly in the reflection.

Casting Wealth and Success Spells

- Cast your circle.

- Set and light the candles and lay the two golden objects.

- In your mind's eye, envision the power of the universe filling that space within the triangle with wealth. Envision the golden objects multiplying right before your very eyes.

- Recite an incantation, calling upon the universe to bring abundance into your life.

- Say these words thrice: "Such is my will. So mote it be."

- Then, using the ring as a pendant, wrap the golden chain around your neck. With this act, you are connecting your energy with the wealth energy of the universe.

- Wear the necklace at all times as your lucky charm.

A Spell to Get the Job of Your Dreams

This spell is to be conducted in the night of the New Moon. Candles are effective in success spells because fire is symbolic of ambition. In order for this spell to work, you need to have a specific goal in mind and a realistic yet optimistic perception of your capabilities.

- Cast a circle.

- Light cinnamon incense.

- Combine the two oils. Then, anoint the candles with the oil from one end to the other.

- Place the brown candles at the center of your circle of protection. On your right side, place the green candle. On your left side, place the white one.

- Light the white candle. While doing this, recite an incantation. Ask the powers of the universe to help clarify your sight, to give you strength to stick to your goals, and to open pathways for opportunity. Say these words with confidence: "Because such is my right."

- Then, light the green candle. While doing this, persuade yourself that luck is on your side and that success is at the tip of your fingers.

- Invite your deity to come to you.

- After that, light the brown candles you've placed at the center. While doing this, see in your mind's eye the opportunity arriving to you. If you're after a particular job, imagine yourself already working that job, sitting behind that desk, wearing that uniform, performing the tasks, reaping the rewards…

- Say this out loud: "As it is real in my mind, so it must be."

- Then, extinguish the candles.

- For seven consecutive nights, light the two brown candles for nine minutes, no more, no less. Then, meditate on your dreams and constantly revisit and reevaluate your goals.

A Spell for Clearing Debts or Unsettled Bills

The purpose of this spell is not to magically make your debts vanish but to attract money in order to help you settle your bills.

- The first thing to do would be to bathe the candle in cinnamon oil.

- Next, fold the copy of the bill. Tuck it beneath the candle holder.

- Light the candle and the cinnamon incense.

- While gazing into the fire, utter your incantation.

- Know in your heart that as the candle burns, it is lighting the way for a money-generating source to find its way to you.

- In your mind's eye, envision yourself paying the bill.

- Focus on the current bill rather than shifting your energy to general wealth.

- When unexpected money does arrive to you, settle the bill immediately. To do otherwise would be to disrespect the spell and to disregard the universe's aid.

Casting Spells for Health

A Spell for Healing Yourself (Injury)

- The first thing you need to do is to arrange the candles in a circle.

- Then, place your picture in the center.

- Fill each of the six candles with the energy of the 4 spirits of the earth.

- Ex: Hold a candle in your hand and say: "I charge thee with the powers of Fire…" *etc.*

- Ask each element to combine their powers to help you heal from your injury.

- Then, light the candles. Say these words: "As I light thee, I ask thee to burn my pain."

- Then utter these words: "From wound and pain, I shall be free."

- Do this spell every night until you are able to recover.

A Spell for Letting Go of a Bad Habit

Use this spell to fortify your efforts in recovering from an addictive habit.

- The first step is to sheathe the addictive substance (ex. a bottle of alcohol, a pack of cigarettes, etc.) with the first piece of black cloth.

- Next, take the black candle and use a knife to engrave a counterclockwise spiral.

- Light the black candle.

- Burn the second piece of cloth. As you do this, express your dislike towards the piece of cloth which symbolizes your addiction.

- Say these words: "I let go of this habit which causes me harm."

- Then, extinguish the fire.

- Bury in the ground the addictive substance wrapped in cloth along with the remains of the burnt cloth.

- Then, perform a ritual of cleansing. You may wash your hands or your face or bathe.

- Afterwards, light the white candle.

- Inhale and exhale deeply three times and tell yourself that you are clean and free.

Wiccan Sex Spell

You have to pour wine on the ground in the course of the spell, so perform it outside if you can, otherwise you'll need to take some soil indoors in a container.

1. Cast a circle, then grasp the rose petals and ask Venus, the Goddess of lust and passion, to bless your circle with her presence. Experience the feeling as the Goddess fills your circle with her energy, then put the petals on the soil (if outside, or in the plant pot if indoors).

2. Place the crystal on the petals, and gaze at it as you visualize your favorite sexual fantasies in vivid detail. Take the time to really feel your fantasies, with all your senses.

3. Grasp the chalice, and request the Goddess for the sex you desire. This works best if it's spoken from the heart, or if you

don't feel confident enough to do that, you may wish to write it down beforehand, then memorize it or read from the paper. Be careful not to name anyone – these spells are not designed to coerce people to do things, although they will draw like minded people to you, who will freely give you the sex you desire.

4. Drizzle the wine slowly over the garnet, and then allow it to be absorbed into the soil - this is your offering to the Goddess. Then thank her for blessing the circle, and make your farewell before closing it. If you've used a plant pot indoors, empty it somewhere outside, preferably in a flower bed, but anywhere that feels right to you. You should now keep your garnet beneath your pillow or close to your bed, and await the outcomes of your spell with eager anticipation!

Spells for Happiness

Everyone deserves to be happy. However, if you are not happy, and you wish to cast spells for happiness, you need to realize that magic cannot be treated as a cure for your problems. You have to be willing to face your problems and deal with them. Keeping in mind that spells only work if you put in some work yourself, so if you're going to cast a spell for happiness, you have to be prepared to make an effort to lift your mood and banish negative thoughts and energy.

Here are some of the best spells for lifting your mood, de-stressing, and generally making your outlook brighter, so that you feel happier.

- Tie Away Your Troubles Spell

- Before you can be happy, you have to get rid of the things that are making you unhappy. A good way to do this is to take a chord and hold it between your hands. Think of a particular thing that is making you unhappy, and allow yourself to be upset and angry about it. Cry if you need to but concentrate on what is bothering you.

- When you feel ready, tie a knot in the middle of the chord. Pull hard on both ends – be angry with the knot, because it represents what is upsetting you. Now set the knot aside, and meditate. Visualize your life without the knot – and the problem it represents – in it. Think how happy you will be. Imagine you are happy right now, and think how much better you feel with the problem out of your life.

- Now take the chord, and untie that not. As you release the knot, your take the bad thing out of your life, and you are able to move on. If you have more than one barrier to your happiness, you can repeat this spell on another day.

Money protection spell

- Start by cleansing yourself and scrubbing yourself with an herb of your choice.

- Now carry all your materials outside with you.

- Take your green or gold candle and place some of the essential oil on your palm and cover the candle in it completely.

- Light it up and allow it to develop a steady flame.

- Close your eyes and call upon your deities that you wish to invoke for your ritual.

- Now place it inside the bowl and cover it with the lid that has the holes.

- Now cover one of the holes with your coin.

- You can ideally place it over the middle hole as it will help the smoke coming out from the other holes surround and cover the coin completely.

- While this happens, you can repeatedly chant "Money gain, No money lost, Let me gain, Let it be, Bring me more, So Mote it be"

- Once done, simply take the lid off and allow the candle to keep burning.

- Take the yellow candle and place it next to the gold or green and light it.

- Replace the lid on top and cover the center hole with the coin.

- Allow the smoke from both candles to cover the coin completely.

- Now chant the saying "Goddess of protection, Please help me, Protect the money you see, And let it be, Thank you"

- Visualize that all your money is safe and that there is no loss. You are able to save the money that you have and it is not being wasted on anything. There is new money coming in and even that is safe and not going anywhere.

- Now close our eyes and blow out the candle and don't open it until the smoke from the candle dissipates.

- Finish the ritual by thanking your deities.

Chapter 20: The Elements Of The Witch's Path

The elements of the path of the witches are also known as the eightfold way. This represents the various methods that the witches are able to use to perform magic. These elements have been in existence since the ancient Wicca days and were reinforced and written down by Gerald Gardner. In his publication dubbed the "Book of Shadows", Gardner recognizes the eight elements, which are detailed in this chapter.

The First Path: Intent

Intent is essentially a short form that denotes intention. In this case, the most important aspect is identified as forming your intent, which means focusing all of your efforts toward a certain goal. All forms of magic, ranging from the power of intention to the law of attraction, are derived from the ability to focus on your intent, which helps in discovering what you may want to achieve.

To arrive at a well thought out intent, you must ensure that you are privy to the following:

- The knowledge of proper visualization skills
- The ability to conduct concentration exercises
- The knowledge of proper meditation
- Knowing your true will
- Ensuring that you stay focused without dwelling on the negativities of what you cannot achieve
- Knowing how to be clear on your wants from the universe, and what to do to ensure that you get them

The Second Path: Trance

Trance refers to a state of altered consciousness where you are awake but in another world. When a person is in a trance state, they are oblivious about all the happenings of the natural world. The ability to enter into this state is considered to be one of the basic skills of witches; they must be able to get in and out with ease. To normal humans, entering a trance state is very strange and scary, although, to the Wicca, it is a daily practice that is really not considered to be complicated once you master it. In as much as non-pagans make trance look like a serious demonic act, the fact remains that it is similar to the feeling that people have when they take alcohol or various drugs. The "high" is more or less the same, with the major difference being that the Wiccan trance is controlled and can easily be exited from.

For the Wiccans, entering into the trance state requires them to prepare for a while and get the necessary tools in order. These tools vary, as some witches can just induce a trance mode naturally, while others require the use of stipulated tools in order to get themselves in the mental state of actually falling into a trance. Notably, you cannot fake trances, and they require cooperation of the mind; conscious and subconscious elements of the brain are required.

Some of the key tools that help facilitate the trance state are as follows:

- Music
- Lit candles
- A flog or whip made up of nine tails
- A bathtub, large basin, or generally a place where you can create the feeling of falling into a deep trance
- Another Wiccan counterpart

The Third Path: Rites, Spells, Charms, Runes, and Chants

This is the most renowned and popular concept that comes to mind when people hear about witches and witchcraft in general. This path is often referred to as the "craft" or the "art of magic", and it summarizes everything that the witches get involved in throughout the course of carrying out their activities. Notably, the craft is not conducted in layman's language, and it is a fact that the chants and spells are normally cast using an unknown language. This is done to provide a sense of identity, as well as to create a sense of performance, which helps in the utilization of all of the senses. Through this strange language, the magician's will and intent are communicated in the subconscious and is believed to be in harmony with the energy obtained from the universe.

As is evident, the spells are quite specific, and the witches know exactly what they are calling upon. There is often great importance in being specific, since the witches believe that the energies are distinct, and calling upon the wrong one, whether mistakenly or not, can be disastrous. The successful implementation of the chants and spells requires a great level of creativity and memorability, and the spells are usually characterized by the repetition of the same words over and over again until whatever is called upon finally manifests itself. The spells and chants are constructed in such a way that they must be stated as they are with no modifications, removal of words, or differences in intonation.

The Fourth Path: Intoxicants

Intoxicants have been used since time immemorial in the witch's arena to achieve a state of trance as well as in the creation of magic. There are many intoxicants that have been cleared for use in most of the Wiccan ceremonies, including the following:

- Incenses and strong smelling plantations

- Herbs of specific kinds; mainly, the witches prefer those that produce a lot of smoke upon being burned

- The use of spices, specifically for the major role of altering the states and physical abilities of the participants so as to achieve certain effects

Commonly abused drugs such as marijuana, tobacco, and alcohol; however, unlike other people who use these substances and get rowdy and out of control, the witches consume them in a very controlled manner and actually use most of them by physically burning them or, in the case of alcohol, pouring it so as to successfully cast their spells. The witches recognize that the reliance on these elements to achieve mystic powers and a higher form of energy is actually retrogressive, as they may end up affecting their abilities more negatively and actually losing their powers. Casting spells requires sobriety and total focus, a factor which is affected by the use of drugs.

Notably, where the invocation of energy and powers is done using intoxicants, there is a very strict rule that is put in place to ensure that no minors are involved.

The Fifth Path: Dances and Sacred Body Movements

This is another common aspect that comes to mind when the concept of witches and witchcraft comes into play. The dances that the witches do are different from those of normal people in multiple ways. First, the movements are not really in rhythm, and the dancers act as though they are in a trance or have been possessed by some form of a spirit. The dancers swing their arms into the air and move in a manner which may be confused as being related to being intoxicated, and it usually happens around a fire in the various ceremonies.

However, the trance dances are not the only ones that exist. Some of the other popular dances include the following:

- Yoga, which is mostly done for meditation purposes
- Systematic dances, which are meant to raise and redirect energy
- Belly dances, which are very sacred and only done during specific events
- Ecstatic dances, which are mainly used to worship the divine
- Circle dances, which are used in all of the Wiccan rituals

- Lead and spiral dances, which are mostly done during gratitude events where giving thanks is to be practiced

The Sixth Path: Blood and Breath Control

For a long time, Wiccans have been known to use breath in conjunction with blood in order to induce and maintain their meditative states. The spiritualists believe that whenever the breath is wandering, the mind is also considered to be unsteady. Therefore, calm breath is an illustration of a calm mind, which makes learning breathing control imperative. It is a basic belief that whenever stable breathing is achieved, the end result is a long life and vice versa. Therefore, Wiccans who wish to live for a long time have the imperative role of learning how to control their breathing process.

Since breathing exercises are vital for Wiccan members, the following techniques are taught in their initial classes as soon as they join:

- The essence of proper breathing and the importance behind it
- Basic breathing techniques, commonly referred to as the Yogic
- Introduction to the whole aspect of chakras and the breathing exercises involved in the said chakras
- Some of the postures that alter or facilitate blood flow

- Sensory deprivation, which is achieved through the various meditation methods

- The concept of the breath of fire used in the raising of energy

In the Wicca traditions, which permit the involvement of children, breathing exercises and control are considered to be a little extreme, and so the system does not really encourage the participation of the said children to prevent putting them at any risk.

The Seventh Path: Scourge

The scourge is considered to be among the most misunderstood and unique magical elements in the Wicca practice. The scourge is usually much more than a tool; it is considered to be a sign of the suffering usually faced on the path to achieving enlightenment. Therefore, this path teaches the importance of embracing any form of suffering that may come your way and using it as motivation to find the proper direction to enlightenment and all its constituents.

To achieve total knowledge of this path, the Wicca priests and priestesses normally teach members from the following from the beginning:

- The examination of some of the periods where the members have faced some form of suffering; the priests always aim at helping the members understand how their season of suffering enabled them to achieve various milestones in their lives or even helped in the improvement of their character

- The importance of creating minor disturbances, sometimes so that the trance state can be induced

- The proper technique and tradition of implementing scourge and the reasons as to why it actually works

Notably, since this path is all about finding positivity in the midst of a highly negative situation, the fact that the leaders required the inducement of a negative occurrence means that children are better off not being involved, as it may affect them psychologically. Therefore, this path is best carried out by adults who have a clear and concise mental state.

The Eighth Path: The Great Rite

The eighth path is also known as the sacred marriage, and it's considered to be a very powerful tool used by the Wiccans to communicate with the divinity. According to the beliefs, a woman was previously at the altar, and it is of pivotal importance to ensure that an altar is erected at specified places.

Some of the concepts that the Wicca are taught in relation to the great rite are as follows:

- The major theory behind the concept of the great rite

- How to balance the energies of yin and yang

- A vital meditation that honors the forces of creation

- How to practice the sex magic theory

- How to draw down the sun and moon

The great rite passage is considered to be of very mature content, and so only adults receive lessons pertaining to it. In the Wicca traditions where children are also initiated, they must first become of age before they receive the lessons.

Chapter 21: The Benefits Of Wicca

Becoming a Wiccan means that you are dedicating your life to being a more positive and focused person. It means that you want to develop strategies to take care of yourself and understand how to be one with nature and everything that exists around you. It's not just about magical spells or creating potions, but rather wanting self-improvement. There are many benefits to being Wiccan. Wicca and witchcraft put an emphasis on using energy from the earth and nature and also bringing the sky and air energy back into the earth. Being a Wiccan is about feeling as though you are one with the earth, with all living things surrounding and embracing you. It's a peaceful religion.

The main aspects of Wicca are what will save the world from human destruction:

- Environmentally friendly people - Aware of the earth. (What affects one thing, will affect all of us, as whatever we do will come back to us threefold.)

- Responsibility - Your words and actions are no one else's fault, even if it feels like they are.

- Honoring our gods and goddesses which make up all matter and all living things.

- Self-respect, and respect for others.

If everyone lived by these principles, the world would be a much happier place. Nature would live on to survive for centuries more. All living things would grow and flourish into a beautiful place where they want to be. There would be fewer problems and more help from our society. This is why Wicca is so beneficial.

The Greatest Things About Being a Wiccan

Wicca is about improving oneself to feel beneficial to the community and to their religion. Wicca teaches self-empowerment while offering others the support they need to feel good in their lives too. The wisest thing a Wiccan lives by is as follows: ***"If it harms none, do as you will."*** This means that you can do as you please as long as you are not harming Earth or anything or anyone around you. Wicca is more about keeping to yourself while focusing on your own happiness and goals and avoiding trying to convert others or getting them to see your side. Just live, forgive, and let go. Some of the greatest things about Wicca are as follows:

Wicca is not judgmental.

It honors and worships divine femininity; everyone is neither male nor female because everyone is seen as equal and as one. The goddess is the center of everything while the masculine traditions offer accomplishments of the sacred gods - Horned God and the Green Man.

Wicca is nature and Earth-friendly.

Wiccans believe that Earth is part of us, and we are part of the earth and all it has to offer. They celebrate food and the gods and goddesses for providing us with all we have, as many cultures are less fortunate. Wiccans have an undeniable connection to all life on Earth.

Wicca honors the physical.

The body, the mind, the soul, food, sex, and the physical aspects of the world are all seen as sacred to Wiccans.

Wicca demands creative independence.

When someone has come up with an idea for the religion, Wicca is too quick to put that into the religion itself. Everyone is open to their creativity, and nothing is set in stone. Wicca has a strong need for poetry, songs, art, inner experiences, etc. It leaves room for mistakes and does not judge anyone for their past or for who they are today. It's about self-love and inner peace.

Wicca cultivates family time and close bonding.

The celebrations like Easter and Christmas are traditional in the fact that they bring families together and help them bond better. Thanksgiving is about appreciation for one another and about giving back to others. Wicca is not a dark religion, nor is it moralistic.

When they hear the name Wicca, right away, many people think about magical spells and Witchcraft. These are the people that don't know much about Wicca and judge based on what's said or what they have heard. Although Witchcraft is part of the Wicca religion, as you have read, it is not everything; however, there are many benefits to the Witchcraft side of things as well.

The Benefits of Witchcraft

No two people, or rather witches, are alike, and no two spells are exactly the same. Witchcraft is all about the energy you put into your spells or potions and not the physical kind of energy. Wiccans are usually light witches and don't practice dark magic due to the law they stand by, which is to harm none. Here are the benefits to practicing Witchcraft:

Anyone can become a witch.

People from all religions, backgrounds, and cultures can practice magic. Wicca is not the only religion that practices it, nor is it the only reason people will do Witchcraft. However, the reason most people think of Wiccans as witches or warlocks is that they are the most known religion that does practice Witchcraft.

No rules.

As with anything or how most things should be in your life, you hold all the control. You can choose to make your own spells; do your research about how to carry out certain things like protection spells or healing spells. However, you can make your Witchcraft as simple or as dynamic as you would like. There are spell books and grimoires out there to help you, there are also guides and tools for you to mix together when learning. Whatever you do though, be careful in how you use your energy because that is the main ingredient. When you are calm and peaceful, your spell will always turn out the way you would like it to. It also doesn't matter about the lunar phases on when your spell will become successful or when you should start. Wiccans use the lunar phases as a guide to do their own thing.

Anytime and any place.

When you get good at Witchcraft, you can make up a spell or chant inside your head anywhere you would like at any given time you feel is appropriate. Wiccans and other witches have designated and sacred places to perform their spells and magic. But the choice is up to you on where you would like to learn, create, and spellbind.

Nature spending.

A ton of spells require certain herbs and also things you may have not heard of before, and so you will be spending a lot of time in nature learning about the balance of the earth. With practice, you will learn how to ask for permission and be able to hear the wind, or feel the trees and soil beneath your feet. Witchcraft is about being aware of your surroundings, developing a strong mind through meditation, and understanding respect for all living things that involve your environment. There is no better place to get peace other than by yourself in a natural setting.

Knowledge.

If you want to do something right or get something perfect, you will have a lot of studying to do. You will find yourself learning about herbs, flowers, roots, teas, potions, spells, and things you didn't think were possible. You will gain knowledge about natural healing, chakra healing, meditation, gems, crystals, myths, history and the magical properties that every living thing holds. The more you know, the more powerful you will become, and the better off you and your Witchcraft will be.

Knowing what you want.

If you are unsure about your passions or your journey as you truck through life, Witchcraft can really show you and teach you things you never knew about yourself. Spell work requires you to have a clear state of mind and a peaceful presence, and so when you do your spells, you have to make sure you are clear on what you want to happen here. As a successful process, doing spells and learning more about Witchcraft will give you insight on yourself and how to reach your most desired goals.

De-stressor.

Practicing Witchcraft is a time where you can focus your mind on what you are doing rather than all the other things life is trying to throw at you. It creates stability within your brain and your soul spirit. Witchcraft helps you reflect on what you have done, and where you are now for the sole purpose of getting your spell right and having it become successful. If your mind is cluttered, so will your spells.

So many paths to choose from.

There are many witches including the sea witch, a hedge witch, a green witch, etc… Each witch has their own unique specialties and practices their Witchcraft a certain way. With the many witches or choices, you have, you can find one that you can relate to with the most, and go down that path. Or you can choose all the paths and see what kind of witch you will be in a few years. The options are endless, and the choice is all yours.

Excuse to celebrate.

The summer and winter solstices are one of the many reasons a witch or warlock will choose to celebrate. For example, at the winter solstice, you may have chosen to be a sea witch (works with water), and create spells to replenish the Earth or soil in the dead months. The many Sabbats are easily celebrated, and no witch misses an opportunity to do their traditional rituals. These rituals may include preparing a feast with certain herbs and natural ingredients, go on nature walks to clear their minds, meditation to open their spirit, honor their ancestors for guidance, and many more.

Inclusive.

Witchcraft can be anyone, it doesn't matter if you are bisexual, trans-sexual, masculine, or feminine. This culture or religion surrounding Wicca is very "everybody friendly." No witch or warlock feels the need to judge, but they will feel the need to support and encourage. It gives people the opportunity to try whatever they have wanted for so long and also promotes kindness, self-love, balance, and internal healing.

Increases healthy habits.

Because Witchcraft uses everything natural, the teas they drink, the food they make, and a lot of time that they spend outdoors promotes healthy habits physically and mentally. Witches spend their free time journaling their adventure, reflecting upon others and themselves, connecting with elements, and taking care of the Earth. They don't make excuses for why they can't do something, and when they have hurt someone unintentionally, they try to express themselves in a way that decreases the conflict.

The bottom line about the many benefits of Witchcraft is that in reality, your main practice is being in touch with yourself while being completely connected to Earth. It's about learning more about yourself and overcoming those unhealthy habits to set yourself up toward your goals. By reading and researching upon Witchcraft, you may come across many spells and techniques that are most comfortable with what you connect to. By going this route, you won't be let down, or find any disadvantages, as Witchcraft is about making mistakes, and then gaining rewards and success from learning from your mistakes. It is an empowering path to choose. With these many benefits comes the power of the mind. With nature comes the health of mental illness. Anxiety is released and mood swings dissipate. As long as you continue to strive for yourself, you will succeed in whichever path you choose.

How to Deal with the Public If They Don't Accept Your Faith

A lot of times, people will judge the unknown or what they don't understand. They may see you as weird or idiotic because you believe in the magic of Wicca. The thing about this religion though, is that as it is helping you feel more empowered, it will also help you with your self-esteem. When your emotions and mind are in check, what others say you can and cannot do is none of their business. There are two ways to go about your faith to Wicca, both are for a number of reasons. One way is that you could hide your faith, put your Wicca books away, and don't tell anyone. The reason for this is you would be afraid to get fired, lose custody of your children, or be discriminated against for your practices. You may keep silent about your given religion because you don't want to indulge in who other Wiccans are as well and ruin their lives. However, this could stem from paranoia about your faith and how people would act. The other way is to be proud of your faith, and whatever happens will happen. You may choose to bring out those books, display your gems and crystals, and give advice or support to those who are down the same path as you. Choosing this route is a free way to be.

Some things to keep in mind is to never ask someone about their religion if they are a Wiccan, some people may find it offensive, and feel judged. If they bring it up, you can show that you are open-minded to the idea, and even ask questions about it. Also, if you happen to overhear someone's thoughts or faith about Wicca, never indulge or "out" them to anyone else, as it is never anyone else's business. It shows respect for the opposing party as well because you don't know if they want to hide it or if they don't care.

In addition to keeping Wicca a secret, many people choose this route because the person likes to preserve their power and energy, and also Witchcraft should be taught by another person, not by the public. This is because Witchcraft should never be used for the intent to harm, and a true Wiccan will know the intent of someone else while teaching them magic. The people who choose to share their faith openly have their reasons because it shows personal empowerment, and courage stemming from physical, mental, and emotional strength. Some Wiccans may feel that hiding their faith goes against the religion itself which makes them feel limited to what they can and cannot do. When you are honest about your faith and open to the possibilities, your craftiness becomes more effective, and you will develop self-confidence on a level you didn't have before. However, most Wiccans choose both sides, they share their faith with close friends and family, but don't openly admit it to the world. Whatever suits you and your needs best is your choice, as there is not a wrong choice in this.

Chapter 22: Healing Powers of Herbs & The Practice of Wicca

The practice of Wicca has a great deal to do with the rituals involved in healing with herbs and other foods. Even the vegetables and meat that you eat has a sacred energy and as you connect more to the plant and animal kingdoms through your practice, you will discover and enjoy the magic of all healing foods and herbs.

For this chapter, we will look at some of the common herbs to get you started with your own Witch's cabinet of healing remedies that are also a good way to promote good health and vitality. Sometimes, depending on what kind of spell you are going to cast, you will not ingest the herbs yourself; they will often just be used to decorate your altar or to set a clear intention that will help the magic of your spells and rituals unfold.

The power of herbs has long been known and humans have been using them to aid their ailments and perform magic for centuries. The techniques we use today in our kitchens are quite similar to the way herbs were prepared long ago; not much has changed, and not much needs to because it is the best way to use the magic of herbal remedies like this.

Witches were persecuted for their knowledge of herbs and how to use them to heal people. Even today, the use of herbs instead of prescription drugs is not widely practiced by the medical industry; however, these little pieces of plant life carry some of the most potent magic on Earth and help with a wide variety of things, in addition to simply using them as a bundle if incense or a bouquet offering on your altar or in your rituals.

The most common herbs in the Witch's cupboard can be found in almost any culinary garden and they have more magic than most people care to know in these modern times. Take a look at the list below and see what herbs you already know and work with that can bring more magic into your life.

Rosemary

This heart shrub has been used for centuries to flavor food with its robust earthiness. It is a potent magical herb as well and can be used to heal a variety of ailments and support the overall health of an individual in many ways. Outside of the body, sprigs of rosemary built into a wreath, or laid upon an altar, offer up a great energy of opening and acceptance. Rosemary, when sniffed, clears the nostrils and opens the mind. It is a sacred plant involved in many rituals of fertility and abundance and has a great way of banishing unwanted energies from the self and the home.

You can dry it or keep it fresh and use it to dispel unwanted spirits, and also as a tonic to help with memory, in spells of fidelity, in rituals of power and protection and for purification. You can use rosemary in your bath water to enhance your sacred bath rituals and you can also decorate parts of your home with it, making it into bouquets and keeping it in fresh water.

Thyme

This culinary herb is more than just for seasoning a roast chicken. It is a dainty herb and has a very feminine nature, unlike the very masculine rosemary. It can be used in a variety of ways and has been known to aid in digestion and as a cough remedy. It can also help with your attitude, promoting a more positive vibration for you. According to some folklore, thyme is a favorite of the fairies who will be drawn to your garden more if you plant thyme in it, promoting more work for you with fairy magic. It has antifungal and antibacterial properties and can be taken as a fresh tea, twice daily, to help with the ailments of the lungs and the digestive system.

Thyme is also beneficial in herbal baths to aid with rheumatism and overall ache and pain in the body. It has been known to ward off nightmares, and a few sprigs under the pillow can help with this energy. For spell work, use time to increase strength and courage. It is also powerful during the Spring to leave behind Winter's chill to embrace Spring's renewal and rebirth.

Sage

This herb is used in casting work to promote long life, wisdom, protection and the fulfillment of wishes. It can be used to help with the grief and sorrow after the death of someone you love. Using sage to make wishes is a common practice for witches and all you have to do is write your wish on a sage leaf, fresh or dry, sleep with it under your pillow and then bury it in the ground the following day. It is an herb of wisdom, healing grief and sorrow, and granting wishes and should be brought into the work you do regularly.

Sage is also one of the most common herbs for "smudging" which is the ritual of smoking away and clearing out energies that are no longer wanted or invited. Smudging can also be used for protection while you do your spell work and ask it to burn and smoke during the course of your rituals. You can make your own herbal sage bundles to smudge with. For healing, it is antiseptic and is a powerful herb for sore throats when gargled. It has also been used to help boost insulin in the body.

Chamomile

This flowery herb is most often associated with the tea you can make from the dried flowers to promote a good night's sleep. It has the ability to calm and soothe the body and promote relaxation of the mind and the muscles in the body. The chamomile flower, when dried and stored, can come in handy in other ways. For spell work, it has been known to work well with casting for money and love. Peace, tranquility, and purification are not far behind but many people are on the lookout for love and money a lot of the time. You can use chamomile in your rituals for these purposes.

You can also drink chamomile as a tea to relax or even add it to your bath water to soothe your muscles and joints. It can be very helpful to aid with digestive discomforts, as well as the healing of skin ailments like cuts and burns when applied topically in a salve or ointment. It is a cleansing and relaxing herb and it will serve many purposes in your rituals, spells and remedies.

Lavender

This beautiful herb is best known for its aroma and is often used as an aromatherapy oil or as a dried herb, put into sachets or small pillows to help promote a relaxed and calm state of mind and feeling of tranquility. In your rituals and spell work, Lavender can be used for fertility, the strengthening of love and to help sharpen the mind.

Using lavender regularly as an essential oil or aromatherapy will help you stay grounded and in balance with your inner harmony of love and peacefulness. It can work well as an incense when dried and burned and so could be used in spell work in this manner to promote these magical qualities.

Garlic

Garlic is very powerful. It has a potent aroma and spicy flavor that has been used frequently throughout history for more than just cooking. It has been used to ward off evil spirits and energy when the cloves are hung in large braids around a doorway. Conversely, it is said that garlic can be used in the same way to attract a lover so make sure you set the right intention when you hang your garlic around the house. It has been known to work well in rituals of breaking spells, exorcising unwanted spiritual energies, invoking desire and passion, and protection, especially from "energy vampires" who drain you of your personal life force with their own.

Garlic is also considered an antibiotic when ingested raw and cut up. It has a powerful healing impact when taken during times of illness or to prevent common colds and flus. Too much garlic can be irritating to the digestive system and it is most powerful when consumed raw. It will always be an important herbal remedy to keep in your kitchen even when you aren't flavoring your food with it.

This list of herbs is just scratching the surface of a wide variety of herbs you can use that are in your common everyday garden. As a rule of thumb, try not to buy your herbs from a grocery store; grow them yourself either in a small garden in your home or in pots and containers. The work you do with herbs is a valuable part of your Wiccan experience. Harvesting, drying, and utilizing your herbs from the seedling up is a great way to help you bond and connect with the energies of the Earth.

If it is not possible for you to grow all of your magical herbs, try finding them in nature and wild crafting. Look for places that these herbs grow and ask permission from the plant to take some of it home for magical uses. You can find an even greater variety of seasonal plants, flowers and herbs in this way.

The next herbs are some that might not seem as common to the everyday cook or kitchen witch but will become very valuable to your Wiccan practices and should be kept around your cupboard for magical uses.

Mugwort

This herb is a must have for any Wiccan. It has the power to open the mind and the third eye to enhance prophetic dreams and visions that will transport you forward on your journey and help you align with spirit. It has been used as an herbal smoke that you can inhale to promote these visions or simply burning it as an incense, or as a smudging stick, can have an equally powerful and less damaging impact on the lungs. Mugwort as an herbal tea is also well worth the effort of drying it and making an herbal tea infusion to be drunk before bed to promote lucid dreaming. You can also sleep with sprigs of Mugwort under your pillow for the same effect. Put in your bath water as well, and have a ritual bath that will offer you visions and help you journey quest with your spirit guides to help you.

Rose Hips

Rose hips are the part of a rose stem that build up after the rose petals and bloom have all fallen away, leaving a hard, round bud that contains high quantities of Vitamin C and other powerful minerals. It is a very healing remedy and kept around the cupboard, it can be very useful during times of sickness or bouts of cold and flu. It is also an inspiring flavor and scent when brewed as a tea and can be very uplifting and dispel depression and anxiety. Rose hips are also well-known to help with the cycles of womanhood and can promote a healthy uterus and menstrual flow. Used as a skin treatment, rose hip oil can feel very soothing to aging and dry skin. Themagic of rose hips in rituals is that is can offer a very strong feminine balance and energy to help you promote love with wisdom and celebrate the power of the goddess energy in all things.

Yarrow

This thick, flat flower has been used medically to treat wounds, both internally and externally. On the outside, yarrow has the ability to staunch the flow of blood when applied to wounds. On the opposite side, when taken internally as a tea infusion, it has the ability to promote and increase blood flow and has been used to help women force blood flow with late menstruation or unwanted pregnancy. Consider that only small doses be used internally, depending on your intention with it. In addition to its connection to blood flow, yarrow as a magical herb to be used in spells and rituals can be a great source of wealth and abundance, drawing prosperity and helping it flow towards you, and also release whatever is stuck and holding back the flow of prosperity in your life.

Arnica

Arnica is a healing herb that is used to treat bruises, sore muscles, and aching joints. It can be used as a topical cream or ointment and can also be used as a tea infusion. Arnica is a must have in your healing cupboard and it will always be useful as a remedy for the musculoskeletal system of the body. Magically, this herb has a powerful potency to protect and empower the body as much as it heals it. Working with the magical properties of arnica in your rituals and spells can bring about an attitude of power and virility as well as a stronger acceptance of your magical abilities and skills. Let it come into your spell work to help your confidence as you embrace and explore the reality and practice of Wicca.

As you continue to explore herbs in your Wicca work, find new ones every day that speak to you. You may want to start your own Wiccan garden to keep your focus on certain herbal magic and every season you can plant a new variety of herbs to explore. You can also forage for them in the wild and learn about what is growing at what time of year and discover the magic of using herbs and remedies seasonally.

The power of the plant world in relation to your Wiccan spell work and ritual is powerful and learning more about the herbs and their qualities will be a great part of your journey of discovery. Picking up a Wiccan guide to herbs to help you delve more deeply into each and every common herb will balance out your tool kit for working with natural magic and will show you the joy and pleasure of your connection to the world of magic that is growing all around you.

Chapter 23: Wicca & The Spirit World

Wicca is a practice and a craft; it is a devotion to nature the energies and divine spirit inherent in all things. To work with Wicca is to work with spirit and so in order to feel open to embracing these attributes and attitudes, it is helpful to know more about how spiritual energies can influence your work and your connection to your spells and rituals.

For many people who are already interested in Wicca and the magic arts, spiritual influence is a given and is easily embraced. But what does it actually mean to have that kind of a connection? Where is it coming from? And why does it happen more openly and frequently when you are casting magic or performing rituals?

It is a beautiful gift to open yourself to the divine magic of the universe and the very practice of Wicca is one of many ways you can incorporate those experiences into your life.

Finding your spiritual connection can take time and practice. If you are not open to it, it won't really want to open to you either. Some people may find it hard to open to spiritual energies due to a lack of faith or a disbelief that it is possible. Honoring that it is possible to become open and available to divine wisdom from other realms is part of the practice of Wicca.

Many of the practices and rituals, as you have read, involve, and incorporate the worship of a deity, a god, or a goddess. The very nature of putting these energetic life forms, or deities, into the cause or power of your ritual is an act of aligning with the spirit world. It has been known to happen that when you engage more openly and fully with certain or specific deities in your Wicca work that you will align with that source energy and feel it in your body, dream about it, have prophetic visions, or even channel the voice of the spiritual energy.

To some, this might sound terrifying, but when you are casting a circle of protection and declaring intentions of aligning only with positive life force energies that seek to cause no harm, then you will be receiving an important, helpful, and uplifting connection with a higher power who is here to guide you. When you invoke spirit, spirit comes to your aid.

There are several different kinds of energies in the spirit world and some of them are directly linked to the elements. There are a variety of fairy folk who correlate to each element (water, fire, earth, air) and can be called upon to help you in your magic work with these elements.

You may also find encounters with spirit guides that take the form of people, gods and goddesses, animals, and even plants or trees, who are ready and available to open up and guide you along your path. Some energies will also be less helpful and more manipulative or trickster-like and so having your circle of protection cast and your protective enchantments ready for your spirit world work will keep you in a safe alignment with all that is benevolent and good.

A lot of your Wiccan practice may be devoted to the energies of psychic power and spiritual awakening and many of us are able to enhance our openness and connection to the spirit world through our openness and enhancement of our spiritual awakening journey through ritual and spell work. Many people find that the more they practice Wicca, the more open energetically they become, opening a channel of communication between the earth plane and the etheric planes of existence.

Everything has potent life force energy and even the energies that are not embodied who exist in the other realms are available to speak to and ask for the guidance of as you do your ritual work. The following spell can be used to invoke your spirit guides to aid you on your path and show you the way:

Honoring Spirit Guides Ritual

You will need the following items for your altar:

- Purple candle(s)- invoking spirit
- Black candle(s)- protection
- A dish of honey
- A dish of salt
- A dish of pure, and/or charged sacred water

- A bouquet of flowers

Chapter 24: Dispelling Common Myths About Wicca

Of course, despite the great advances that Wicca has made in becoming a legitimate, accepted modern religion, there are still many misunderstandings and prejudices regarding this peaceful, nature-worshipping faith.

Wiccans do not believe in or acknowledge a "devil", or Satan character.

The Wiccan Horned God is symbolic of the virility of nature and of the masculine, it has nothing to do with any Christian notion of evil or of the devil. They believe in the ebb and flow of the natural world, and that sometimes there is growth, and sometimes decay, but darkness is not evil it is simply the absence of light. As they worship the departure and return of the Sun God, so do they commit themselves to the faith that even in the darkest hour, so will Light return to the world.

Wiccans disregard moral absolutes.

They strive to practice their magic and their faith with a portion of humility, never seeking power over another or practicing magic that aims to directly harm or disable someone else.

Wiccans and other pagans do not seek to recruit others

For Wiccan is not a cult. It is a calling to those who wish to pursue its path, and Wiccans take personal choice very seriously.

Wiccans do not sacrifice animals.

That would directly contradict their law to "Harm None". Wiccans do not take the energy from another person in order to make their magic powerful. Wiccans and other pagans believe that we are all imbued with divine energy, as well as the potential to utilize that energy in order to practice magic and witchcraft.

Witches aren't real.

Of course they are; a witch is simply a person who practices magic. (Some Wiccans and witches prefer to spell magic with a "k", i.e. magick, in order to differentiate it from performative stage magic. Either spelling is acceptable). A witch is a self-aware scholar of ways both ancient and modern to utilize the power of the natural world and of themselves to make changes in their lives and in themselves.

You are not a "real" witch or Wiccan without years of commitment and training.

This is a personal choice; you're a witch if you practice magic, and you're a Wiccan if you decide that you are, it's as simple as that. Some Wiccans prefer to pursue their path alone, and we call these individuals "solitary" witches. Others feel more comfortable surrounded by a formal community, and to be taught by ordained elders, priests, and priestesses. There is no wrong way to be a Wiccan, so long as you adhere to the Wiccan Rede and try to practice Wiccan tenets throughout your daily life.

Conclusion

You have finished the book. You should by now have a deeper understanding of what you didn't know before. Everything right now must be exciting and new. Can you wait to get started? Or is this not for you? Did you get all your questions answered? The purpose of this Wicca book for beginners was to help you understand Wicca and what it means to be a Wiccan. It was not to convert you into this religion but to show you that whatever path you choose to undergo; the choice should always be yours.

In this book we have learned the many spells you can practice - of course not all of them. We learned what witches use or write in their Book of Shadows. If you are not appreciative of the practice and promise to always work on yourself and treat others with kindness and the respect they deserve, then you are not following the ways of Wicca. Remember, Wicca is all about self-love and spiritual growth.

The more you work to understand Wicca, nature and the Divine, the more you'll continue to grow wiser and stronger in body, mind and spirit.

The best way to know if Wicca is the best religion for you is to continue educating yourself in the principles and concepts of Wicca while staying aware of your own beliefs and perspectives.

The next step is to apply this set of knowledge and skills to improve your life and those of others. Practice with these basic spells before moving on to more advanced spells. May you have the strength and the courage to use this wisdom for good. Blessed be.

May you use the knowledge you have acquired in this book for good use. As a matter of fact, this is how you can begin to keep your own Book of Shadows. Write out your experiences and the spells that worked for you. Continue to read and search further to grow your knowledge and wisdom.

You are on your way to discovering how to begin practicing Wicca in your everyday life and can now reap the benefits of what you sow through your spell work, casting, intentions, power of three-so mote it be, and so much more. This book is here for you to continue using as a guide to help you grow and evolve more into your spiritual path with this herbal and elemental magik.

All you have to do is embrace the tools, use your intuition, let nature be your guide and open yourself to the possibilities of all that surrounds you in the world of the divine. Any work you do with your Wiccan spells will have an impact on your life. Your energy is always working towards some kind of goal and so while you are practicing this work remember to keep your intentions clear, focused, good-natured, and full of love and light.

Wicca Spells

Discover The Power of Wiccan Spells, Herbal Magic, Essential Oils & Witchcraft Rituals For Wiccans, Witches & Other Practitioners of Magic

Sofia Visconti

Table of Contents

Introduction

Wiccan Practices and Beliefs

Wicca and the Bible

Chapter One: Getting Started

What to Consider When Casting Spells

Protective Circle

Steps to Cast the Wiccan Protective Circle

Secrets to Successful Spell-Casting

Chapter Two: Practices

Ritual Practices

Sex Magic

Wheel of the Year

The Extended Wheel of the Year

Rites of Passage

Wicca Symbols and Signs

Chapter Three: Types of Magic

White Magic

Casting Spells

Red Magic

Black Magic

Chapter Four: The Book of Shadows

British Traditional Wicca

Non-Traditional Wicca

What You Should and Shouldn't Write in Your Book

Chapter Five: Love and Relationship Spells

Red Candle Spell

Ribbon Spell

Rose Spell

Fairy Love Spell

Love Poppet

Kiss the Moonlight - A Strong Love Charm

Love Star

A Love Pouch With a Magnetic Lodestone

Chapter Six: Money and Wealth Rituals

Rice Ritual

An Abundance of Money Ritual

Water Ritual

Green Candle Money Ritual

Pumpkin Spice For More Cash

Pay a Bill

Wealth Attraction Bath

Welcome Wealth Spell

Chapter Seven: Health and Wellbeing Spells

Energy Spells

Chapter Eight: Magic and the Law of Attraction

Chapter Nine: Protection Spell

Chapter Ten: Other Spells

Healing Spells

Power of Three

The Healing Charm

Candle Spells

Candle Melding Love Spell

Return to Me Candle Spell

Flames of Progress

The Light of Three

Reuniting The Reflections Spell

Safe Revenge Spell

Find a New Job

Chapter Eleven: Crystals and Magic

Types

Choosing the Right Crystal

Rituals

Chapter Twelve: Wicca Herbal Magic

Elemental Power of Plants

Conclusion

Introduction

Wicca is mostly practiced in the West and has its roots in the occult. It is a modern movement based on pagan beliefs and practices common in Northern and Western Europe before Christianity became the religion people followed. It is mostly girls, and women follow Wicca since the focus of the religion is on goddess worship and female power. Wicca comes from the word wicce, which means "to bend or shape nature to your service," and this is the basis of this practice. Wiccans cast spells or perform rituals only when their intent is to make changes in the physical world. They often use spells for protection, healing, fertility and to banish negative influences.

Most people are unaware of this religion, and some have developed a fear of it because they are unaware of what it actually is or have been told false or misleading information about it.

There are some who are brave enough to follow this religion, and research shows that there are over 10,000 witches in the country. Research shows that many people now choose to follow Wicca, Pagan and neo-Pagan religions. According to the Pagan Federation, there are over 100,000 people who follow various Pagan rituals and practices.

I have explained the various aspects of Wicca, and its practices and beliefs in my best-selling book, *'Wicca for Beginners: Discover The World of Wicca, Magic, Wiccan Beliefs, Rituals & Witchcraft.'* Many readers have requested additional content on spells and magic, so in this book, *"Wicca Spells: Discover The Power of Wiccan Spells, Herbal Magic, Essential Oils & Witchcraft Rituals. For Wiccans, Witches & Other Practitioners of Magic'* I will delve deeper into the realms of wiccan magic.

Wiccan Practices and Beliefs

Wicca is a practice that recognizes two divinities – the Horned God or God and the Goddess, which means it is a theistic practice. In traditional Wicca practices, God is the primary deity. In the feminist or modern approach of Wicca, the goddess is the primary deity. Some groups also recognize the goddess as the only deity. The guard is associated with forests and sun while the goddess is associated with the sea, stars, and moon. The latter is also known as the mother goddess. The followers of this movement focused on one or both deities and the elements of nature during their worship. The practices of divination, incantations, and witchcraft are some significant practices of Wicca.

Some detailed and specific Wiccan beliefs are slightly hard to identify since there is no authoritative or singular book that any Wiccan lives by. Many different groups use this religion or practice. Wicca does not adhere to any specific truth or doctrine but focuses more on how the individual practices the religion in the form of rituals, witchcraft, ceremonies, etc. Having said that, most followers of this practice adhere to some basic practices and beliefs.

● Every Wiccan observes annual holidays or Sabbats with ceremonies and rituals.

● They respect and worship all the elements – air, water, fire and earth, and spirit, which is the first element. According to Wicca, the spirit is present in every element.

● Wiccans do not believe that magic is supernatural. They believe that magic is the intentional manipulation of the various elements.

● Another common Wiccan belief is that they should not harm themselves or others.

● Wiccans also do their best to uphold the Threefold Law, and this law is based on karma. During any ritual, a witch may emit some magic or energy, and according to the Threefold Law, this energy returns to the witch three times.

● Since the Wiccan religion is open, it does not believe in evangelizing people. This practice accepts other religions and borrows some rituals and practices from them.

● According to the Wiccan religion, people are either reborn or reincarnated after death.

Occult and Wicca

Modern Wicca is influenced by Aleister Crowley, Doreen Valiente, and Gerald Gardner. This is rooted in the occult, referring to various matters that involve the action or influence of various supernormal and supernatural phenomena or powers.

Wicca and the Bible

Worship the Lord Alone

Wiccans always honor the Wiccan deities and the natural elements. The Bible, however, teaches people that they must worship only God and not his creation, according to Exodus 20:3, Psalm 104, and Luke 4:8. Wiccans, however, believe in creation worship, and this is not new. The Apostle Paul was disappointed with this behavior, and he lamented in Roman 1:25, and said, "They exchanged the truth about God for a lie, and worshiped and served created things rather than the Creator—who is forever praised. Amen."

The Lord is Sovereign

Wiccans rely only on the power they find in themselves, other spiritual forces of nature. The Bible, however, forbids this. According to Deuteronomy 18:9-13 and Leviticus 19:31, this act is not only forbidden but is also futile since the Lord possesses complete power and control over everything in the universe. This means that an outcome accomplished through a spell or ritual is often a trick designed to deceive any person and deviate his focus from God. This deceiver will be thrown into an eternal lake of fire, and must never be sought after or followed.

The Lord is the Truth

People who practice Wicca are always asked to do whatever they want, as long as they do not harm any individual. Their actions must never cause harm to anybody, including themselves. This rule is, however, impossible to keep since nobody knows the full effect of their actions. The Wiccan Rede says that practitioners can do what they want, but harm is a relative concept.

Now that you have a basic idea about what Wicca is, let us dive into the world of witchcraft and magic. This book has all the information you need to know about Wicca and teaches you the basic rules you must adhere to. It helps you learn more about how to protect yourself and the people around you when you cast a spell. You'll also learn a few spells you can use to improve your physical and mental wellbeing, attract love and friendship, and protect yourself and your home.

All the information in the book is explained in simple terms, and the spells explained in the book are broken down into step-by-step instructions. So, if you want to change your life for the better without causing harm to anybody else, then consider a Wiccan spell to help you make that change. Regardless of whether you are a beginner or a Wiccan looking for new spells to add to your book of shadows, you do not have to look any further. This book has everything you need to satiate your desires.

Chapter One: Getting Started

What to Consider When Casting Spells

Always Use the Wiccan Rede

According to the Wiccan Rede, you can do anything you want as long as your actions do not cause any harm to people around you. People interpret this statement in different ways. They may also ask the following questions:

1. What does it mean to harm someone?

2. Who should we not harm?

The bottom line is that spell casters must always take personal responsibility for their actions. If you are unsure of what your actions will amount to, make sure to keep your intentions simple and clear.

Never Cast Spells to Manipulate Others

This comes from the point above, and it tells us there may be times when we may want to change the way someone behaves. When we do this, we may cause harm to them. Never use your spells to change how someone thinks, behaves, or acts. You shouldn't do anything to influence their decisions. If you deal with someone who abuses or harasses you, and if the person is toxic, then you should do your best to help them understand the consequences of their actions. You can also wish for you or them to find realization and success away from each other. It is always best to seek justice and not revenge. Always let the universe provide them their punishment.

Do Not Cast Spells on Behalf of Others

It is always good to use your powers to help people around you, but you must do it responsibly. If you do want to cast spells on behalf of others, ensure that you obtain their permission before you do that. Never impose your practices and beliefs on people around you. Give the person enough space, so they come to you and ask for help. Do not attempt any spiritual work on people without their permission.

Keep Your Work Private

There is some meaning behind the superstition, "If you tell people what you wished for, it will not come true." Witches could never talk about their powers or spirituality openly for many years since they were afraid of being punished or persecuted. People now talk freely about their beliefs and practices, but people need to respect others. They must never boast about their spiritual practices, especially when nobody has asked about them. Let us understand why you should not do this. When you tell someone about what you want to do, their feelings about the practice may interfere directly or indirectly with your practice. You need to ensure that you always perform your magic in safe or private places. Within a circle or coven of trust, people can share their energy if they work towards the same intentions or goals.

Protect the Environment and Nature

Always use biodegradable tools and materials whenever you perform any spells. This helps you reduce your carbon footprint. When you clean after yourself, disposing of everything you use for your ritual, ensure you are conscious about how you do this. Make sure to always clean up after yourself when you perform magic in nature. The best thing to do is always to purchase ethically sourced or fair trade ingredients. It is best to purchase these ingredients locally or try making tinctures or grow your herbs at home.

Be Safe

If you want to use candles when you cast spells, make sure they are placed in sturdy holders. Do not place them close to a window with curtains or blinds to avoid fire hazards. Never leave lit candles unattended. If the candle needs to be left burning throughout the night, enclose it in a container or place it on a heatproof dish.

Stay Protected and Cleanse Yourself

If you feel any energy blockages or disturbances when you perform spells, you must regain your spiritual balance. To do this, think about using bath spells or spiritual cleansing. When you cleanse your body and personal spaces, such as your home or workplace, you can protect yourself from any negative energies or psychic attacks. You can prevent these regular interactions.

Look After Yourself

Healthy minds and healthy bodies go together. If you experiment with essential oils, infusions, potions, or similar, make sure you are careful. Remember that magical practices are not meant to be used in place of proper medical attention. If you think you have a health issue, you must speak to a physician or healthcare provider. Do not leave it to the universe to take care of your problems.

Pre-Ritual Protection

One of the best ways to remove the energy that exists in your space is by using a basic ritual. You can also protect yourself when you cast spells by creating a protective circle. This circle helps to create a space where you can work with high energy. You can increase the strength of the spells you cast based on your intent. Most people create a protective circle before they invoke external forces, energy, or spirits. As a newbie to this, there's no need for you to cast that circle for every ritual. You only need to do this when you need additional protection, control, and focus. Always cast a circle, in particular, when you are going to be working with forces beyond your control. You can channel the energy and enhance it using your circle.

Protective Circle

Protective circles come in all sizes and shapes. Some witches or spell casters cast a sphere, while others look at it only as a circle. Some also choose to cast a triangle, star, or square within the circle. It is best to cast the circle before you begin your ritual since this helps to put you in the right frame of mind. How your spells are cast depends on the following:

- Experience

- Personal beliefs

- Personal preference

Expert practitioners only need to visualize the circle.

Steps to Cast the Wiccan Protective Circle

Determine How Much Space You Need to Perform the Ritual

Cast a big enough circle that you can comfortably move about in when you perform the ritual or cast the spell. If you need to cast the circle, so only you perform the ritual or cast the spell, ensure the circle is big enough to allow you to stretch your arms and legs as far as you can. If you want to move or stand in the circle while you perform the ritual, you must create a larger circle. You should visualize this area using the right stones, rope, candles, chalk, or sand, to demarcate the circle.

Cleaning Your Spell-Casting Area

Your spell-casting or ritual circle must be tidy as it is a symbol of integrity and purity. The circle ensures your safety, so use a vacuum or broom to sweep the area free of debris or dirt. To make certain that the area is clean, remove all negativity by purifying it. You can do this in a few ways; spread salt or saltwater around the area, use incense, use a ritual broom to sweep it, play an instrument of some kind, or use a white sage smudge stick.

Preparing Your Tools and the Altar

Once your area is clean, it's time to prepare your tools and get your altar ready. It doesn't matter what you use as your altar; any surface will do, even a table. You don't even need to buy anything special. If you want, you can cover the floor in front of the altar with a cloth; if it works for you, go for it. Make sure that your altar and the cloth, if you use one, is placed centrally in the circle.

When your altar is placed, you must keep in mind that the objects and materials you use are representative of the directions and the elements, so think carefully when you choose what to use. However you set it up, the cardinal points must be clear; you don't want any confusion when you are performing your ritual or casting spells.

Drawing Your Protective Circle

When you draw your circle around the altar, you can use an Athame, a wand, or your fingers. Whatever you use to draw the circle does not need to touch any surface; you can draw it in the air, if you want, as long as it is a full circle.

Before you begin, stand, close your eyes, and inhale deeply. Relax your body and mind, visualize the energy building up in your body to protect you, increasing with each breath you take. Direct that energy into your dominant hand and arm. Focus on the tool you are going to use to draw your circle; visualize the energy going into it from your hand. See the energy leaving the tool and laying in a protective circle.

You don't have to draw the circle just once; some prefer to draw it a few times. You may, for example, want to draw a circle to protect you, draw it again to provide concentration and again for energy. You can draw as many circles as you need, depending on what you need, or you can draw one circle that encompasses everything. You must always visualize your circle and how to keeps you safe from negativity.

Invoking the Elements

Some witches require the elements and cardinal directions to cast spells, and some rituals also require the spirits and the Divine presence to be invoked. Consider this when you are casting your circle; the elements should be set as follows:

● The air element is invoked in the East. Light incense and place it so it faces East.

● The water element is invoked in the West. Fill a glass with water and place it facing West.

● The fire element is invoked in the South. Place a white candle facing South. White candles are symbolic of the fire element and also provide extra protection.

● The earth element is invoked in the North. Place a bowl of salt facing North.

When you have placed your symbols accordingly, stand in the circle and raise your arms, Close your eyes and say, "I ask God and the Goddess to bless the circle. Within it, I am free and protected. So be it."

Or you can say, "I conceive this circle as a place of contemplation and protection. A space between worlds and time outside time. Bless you."

Once you have spoken the words, your circle is ready for you to perform your ritual or cast your spell.

Opening the Circle to Complete the Ritual

Once your spell is cast, you must complete your ritual by opening the circle, using your wand or Athame. Holding it in your hand, move the wand or Athame in the direction opposite to the one you cast the circle with, this will open the circle. At the same time, say, "I am opening this circle, but I am not breaking it." Or you could say, "I undo this circle; I want to leave this place as it was before the spell was cast."

At all times, show due respect to the nature spirits or the deities summoned when your spell was cast. Always thank them for ensuring the success of your spell, show them honor for helping you. Lastly, extinguish the candles and step out of your circle.

A Few More Tips

● Your protective circle is a sphere of energy. It is powerful, but that power depends on how strongly you visualize it. Keep yourself calm and relaxed by using visualization techniques; the calmer you are, the stronger your focus will be.

● Make sure that you have all your tools and elemental symbols before you begin. The last thing you want is to leave your circle because you forgot an ingredient.

● When it comes time to close the circle, make sure nothing enters or leaves the circle. If you need to interrupt a spell, you must visualize a door or window in your circle. When you enter or leave the circle, do so by this opening and always close it after. Make sure the opening is always facing in the correct direction; that way, when you go through it, you are not interrupting your circle.

Understanding Your Circle

The protective circle you cast is a kind of barrier, keeping you safe from the influence that comes from outside it. Negative energy can get in the way of your concentration, breaking your focus, and this is why many people choose to draw a circle to meditate in; it leaves them free to focus fully on their intent.

If you are practicing at home and a door or a window is opened, your circle will stop the energy disappearing through the opening, and it stops energy from another person interfering with your rituals and spell-casting.

If this is your first time casting a spell, it is natural to feel some anxiety. Your circle is a protective bubble around you, keeping you safe. Inside this circle, you can experiment with casting different spells, and nobody else will be affected. If you want to break your circle, walk carefully across the line, and dismiss the circle. This is important and should never be omitted from your rituals.

Summing Up

Many people opt to use witchcraft, spells, and magic when they want something specific. It could be providing protection for them or their loved ones, attracting good health, money, even the job of their dreams. The spells you cast are classed as "white" magic and are positive. They are designed to help you bring about improvements in life, but they can only work if you carefully follow the guidelines.

Never be scared of trying something, keep your focus on your intent, and ensure your ritual area, your body, and your mind are always clean.

Protective circles are drawn so you can perform meditation, witchcraft, and rituals. Make sure you are familiar with your rituals and spells; never try to do one blind, as it were. Always choose the correct words that will ensure your intent is clear to the universe.

The magic circle has two primary functions:

1. It provides protection for you and anyone around you from negative energies;

2. The energy you channel is held safe within the circle.

Your energy must be contained within the circle until you have finished the ritual. To end the spell, always open your circle to release the energy.

Every witch works differently, and not all witches use protective circles. You must do what is comfortable and right for you.

Secrets to Successful Spell-Casting

Confidence in spell-casting comes with practice and experience, and you won't always be in the right mindset to cast a spell, either. When your mindset or your thoughts change negatively, stop. Do not cast any spells or perform any rituals as there is the potential for them to go wrong or not work at all. The following tips can help you be successful:

Secret #1: Don't Worry That Might Not Work

I realize that may not always be possible, but it's a fact that the more you worry about something going wrong, the more likely it is to go wrong. You may be worried about what would happen if the spell went wrong, or if it would even work. Stop, because this is not putting you in the right frame of mind. Learn to see magic as a way of applying intent and energy. Too much time spent worrying about the spell-casting can lead to negative energy getting in the way of your intent.

Let's say, for example, that your spell is all about finding a decent job. It may take you half an hour to focus your energy and your intent on the spell but willpower will add to the power, making it incredibly powerful. That's all well and good, but if then spend the next few days worrying incessantly over whether the spell will work, all you are doing is directing your energy toward the worry, taking it away from your intent – that spells failure.

The solution is quite simple – stop worrying. Have some faith in yourself and your spells and magic. If you are not in a place where you can trust your spells or magic, you cannot get to where you want to. Always remind yourself that your worry is counterproductive. If you catch yourself worrying about the outcome of a spell, tell yourself to stop. The magic works, and you should avoid disturbing it. Let the magic do its job.

Secret #2: Don't Stress About Details

Did you ever find yourself in a situation where you realized that you were out of olive oil and had to substitute almond oil or stumbled over an incantation? There is so much to learn about spell casting that you might find yourself somewhat overwhelmed. Do not worry; take things slowly and remember that magic is about your intentions, and every step, action, or tool involved when you cast a spell is the best way to channel your energy and solidify your intention.

Almond oil may not align with your intentions as olive oil would, but when you pour enough energy and focus on the oil, you can get the job done. It is tricky to substitute herbs or oils in complex spells, and you may not learn what works for you until you tinker with it. So, do not worry. Always try different substitutions and see how the spell works. If you do not like the results, you can change the elements that do not work for you.

In the same way, forgetting what you were supposed to say or stumbling over a few words in a spell or incantation is not the end of the world. Some witches and spell casters have a stutter, and they can still cast spells. There are times when you will struggle to make it through an incantation. Do not let this frustrate you and ruin the spell.

You need to accept that mishaps happen, and they do not affect the spell that much. You have to understand that every incantation is only about intent. If you are focused on your energy and intent the entire time, the spell will work even if you say a string of nonsense. Always give yourself a break when it comes to small details. You can strive to be perfect when you cast a spell, but do not let imperfect casting make you feel you cannot get it right.

Secret #3: Give Yourself Time to Get into your "Witch Mode"

It takes most people a lot of time to switch from one mode to another. For instance, some may find it difficult to switch from the work mode to time-off mode, and from the usual mode to the witch mode. It is difficult to make this transition, especially if you lead a busy life, and it is recommended that you do not override these transition periods. When we try to skip from one activity to another, we often deny ourselves the necessary space to switch into our witch mode.

The skills you use at work or school are not the skills you can use to cast spells or perform any other activity. People believe they can behave like computers, but what they forget is they are not built that way. Our minds need some time to switch from one task to the next, to change between different skills to your spiritual skills. You need to give yourself enough time, so you can make the transition before you cast the spell.

If you cannot make this transition easily or are impatient, you must create a ritual to ease the process. You can try to perform some activities before you cast a spell, and perform these activities any time you want to cast spells. You can make this process simple or elaborate, depending on your needs. You can take a bath or meditate for a few minutes before you cast a spell.

Regardless of what your ritual entails, you need to ensure it is the same ritual you follow before you cast a spell. Your mind builds a connection between spell casting and the ritual, and you can make the transition faster and easier in the long run. It does take some time to implement this ritual, so always give yourself enough space and time so that you can get into the right frame of mind.

Secret #4: Remember to be Theatrical

Since spell work is a personal endeavor for most people, most standard methods are often flat. One of the best ways to move past this is to use psychodrama. This process is where you fake the spell using theatrics. You can dress up, put on some music, create an ambiance that looks witchy, and get into character. You can then perform any spell of your choice. It is always about setting the stage so that you can get into the right mindset. You must create an environment where you feel witchy.

This may feel fake and dramatic initially, but over time, you learn to use these theatrics to cast spells and notice you can produce the necessary results even with these methods. These theatrics help you find the magic within yourself and use it when you cast spells. This is a key factor for most people and helps them silence any doubts they have about their powers.

When you are in character and in a witchy environment, you soon lose yourself in the process. You find that you obtain the necessary results, and the results are better than when you use regular methods. Do not be under the misconception that you must stick to conventional methods or ideas. Always do what you think makes you feel witchy. Use methods or elements that help to set the right mood.

Chapter Two: Practices

If you are a beginner, there are some aspects you must bear a few practices and points in mind.

Ritual Practices

If you are a beginner, always start off small. Try to incorporate some of the rituals mentioned in this section into your routine. This helps you develop a ritual or practice the works best for you. You need to ensure that you develop a routine you want to stick to.

Light a Candle

Most witches and spellcasters say that lighting a candle helps to both calm and center their energy. Try to light a candle when you wake up in the morning while you do your makeup, on your desk at school or work, or even before you go to bed. A sense of calm spreads through your mind and helps to relax you.

Hold a Crystal

One way to connect with various magical tools is to hold them in your palms and focus on their energy. When you want to purchase a crystal, hold it in your palms for a few minutes and focus on the energy in the crystal. You can also meditate to connect with the energy in the crystal. Once you select your crystal, place it under your pillow.

Stir Your Coffee or Tea Counter-Clockwise

If you drink coffee or tea every morning, stir in the counter-clockwise direction using a spoon. This helps to remove any negativity from your day.

Perform Surya Namaskar

Surya Namaskar or sun salutation is a yoga practice that you can perform anywhere. To do this, follow the steps given below:

- Take a deep breath and exhale while you join your palms at the heart center

- Take another deep breath and raise your hands above your head

- Exhale and slowly bend forward. Make sure to keep your knees straight and try to touch your toes. If you are flexible, you can also move your forehead closer to the knees

- Take another breath and shift your hands so your fingers touch the floor in front of your toes. Lift your head up and look forward

- Exhale and bend your head towards your knees

- Take another deep breath and slowly raise your body and lift your arms above your head

- Exhale and bring your hands to your heart's center.

You can perform this sequence as often as you want at home, in whatever room of the house you feel comfortable in

Use Essential Oil Rollers

If you love essential oils, you can carry a glass bottle filled with the oil of your choice. Make sure the bottle has a rollerball. This is a handy piece of equipment to keep in your purse or at your desk. When you need to focus or require a pick-me-up, apply a little oil behind your ears and on your wrists. Inhale the aroma of the oil.

Drink a Cup of Tea

The drinking team is a powerful ritual to keep yourself calm and be mindful. When you choose the herbs or blend for tea, heat the water and watch the tea brew, inhale the aroma and focus only on your breath to calm your mind.

Develop a Skincare Ritual

When you apply moisturizer or sunscreen on your skin, take a moment for yourself and be mindful and quiet. Always pay attention to the process and find a way to calm your thoughts while you apply moisturizer.

Draw Temporary Signs or Sigils

If you love working with runes, symbols, and sigils, draw them for luck or protection in temporary ways. You can draw them on the mirror using face cream, using a spoon while you cook or in your tea or coffee.

Read About Your Day

Find a book or application that tracks all the astrological information about your sun sign. Spend some time every morning to read the predictions, and you do not have to do this for more than five minutes. Just read what kind of energy you may experience during the day.

Focus on the Seasons

You must always be aware of the seasons and their passing. The Wheel of the Year is a huge part of a Witch's path, and we will look into that a little later in this chapter. When you go for a walk or look out the window, you become more mindful of the changes in the seasons.

Sex Magic

Most people are under the impression that sex magic is a kinky term. Some people may relate sex magic to an image of a woman standing naked in front of a fire or cauldron and calling to the universe to bring back her love or to help her find love. Skye Alexander, the author of 'The Modern Guide to Witchcraft,' said this is not what sex magic is. She mentioned that sex magic is not about enhancing or improving one's sex life, but it is something else entirely.

What is Sex Magic?

As mentioned earlier, magic is all about intention. If you want to cast a spell, all you must do is think positively about the spell and be mindful of what you want. The only difference between magic and sex magic is that in the latter, you use sex to practice mindfulness. Through sex magic, you can increase your dynamic sexual energy and creativity and use that to fuel your spells and intentions. The essence of sex magic is to harness your sexual experiences and the emotions you feel during the experience, including the expectation, tension, pleasure, and happiness that comes with having sex, to focus only on your intentions and desires. You can think about sex magic in the following way – when you blow out your candles on your birthday, you are excited to make a wish. Instead of using excitement to make the wish, you use the pleasure of sex to let the Universe know your intentions. This is sex magic.

Western culture has adopted the use of magic in different areas and aspects of life. The magic used in this culture is intended to attract something or create some kind of outcome in the spell caster's life. Sex magic is quite popular among witches now, but it does have ancient roots. Historical texts and excerpts show that sex magic and sexual practices were quite common in the earlier days, and these practices were accepted and widespread than they are today. Rome and Greece have evidence of sex magic, and there is some proof that people in India and China also used to practice sex magic. Since both sex and magic became a taboo, people never practiced it openly. When people used sex magic, they were happy and were able to stay mindful and positive about what they want in life.

How to Perform Sex Magic?

You must focus quite a bit if you want to use your orgasm as a source of energy for magic. The most important thing to remember is to never rush to the finish line. Try to lengthen the process and see what happens during the entire experience. Understand your emotions and feelings. Skye recommends that people should slow their experience down when they have sex and reach the brink of an orgasm at least three times before they allow themselves to come. People need to enjoy the experience fully and move towards the finish line but stop themselves when they near the end of the line and push back. They should relax and repeat the process again.

Before you have sex, you must set the goal or intention. Ask yourself whether you want to attract money, success at work, heal from heartbreak, attract love, or prevent something from happening in your life. You need to bear this goal in mind during the process. Let us assume you want to attract money, so you must hold this intention in mind when you have sex. After you bring yourself to the brink of an orgasm thrice, finally let go with the intention clear in your mind. Release the energy with the thought in mind and allow yourself to come. You send the intention out into the universe using the same energy to project and release the thought. Once you reach an orgasm, stop thinking or worrying about the intention and let it go.

This gives rise to the question – "How do I think about attracting money when I am about to orgasm?" There are ways to help you focus and make it easier for you to enhance the experience. Many people find it easier to draw images and stick those images within their sights. They can use either tape these images to the ceiling or wall and can look at them before they come. This way, they only focus on the image and intent when they come and do not think about anything else. Some also choose to draw pictures of the intent on their partner's body when they have sex. Others use aromatics, such as lavender oil, frankincense, lemon, and peppermint, to help them concentrate.

Whom Can You Perform Sex Magic With?

It is absolutely fine if you do not have a partner. You do not always need a partner to perform sex magic. You can harness the power and intensity of your sexuality without someone else. You can also do sex magic with those people who are not committed to you as your partner. You can also perform this type of magic with someone you do not love. Skye recommends that you always choose a partner whom you respect. You also need to make your intentions clear when you have sex with the person. There is a lot of respect and trust involved for your partner during the process. You are using this experience to manifest an intention or thought that matters to you. When your mind is clear and more focused on your intentions, you can manifest your thoughts more easily. So, it is best to let your partner know what you want to do, so the process works for you.

Always set the intention together. You should discuss your intentions and thoughts with your partner and let them know what you want to achieve. This way, you both work towards the same goal, and otherwise, you may end up doing different things or wanting different things during the process. The goal of sex magic becomes blurry, and this makes it hard to manifest your intention. Always enter the experience respectfully so that you can manifest your intention positively. It is also okay if the process does not work for you. When you go through the process of sex magic, you end up having some amazing sex regardless of whether you could manifest your intentions in the universe. When you choose a partner you trust, communicate your needs, and make the experience long, sensual, and slow, you are in for a great experience. So, why not try it?

Wheel of the Year

The Wiccan practice is quite flexible, but there is one important element that every Wiccan must follow – the Wheel of the Year, the structural center of the Wiccan practice, or religion. There are eight holidays in the Wiccan year, known as the Sabbats, and these provide Wiccans with occasions to come together with other Wiccans, whether it is to have an informal celebration or to perform coven rituals.

Since Wiccans are solitary practitioners, they know they join their energy with the energy of millions of other practitioners across the globe when they perform their Sabbat rituals.

The Sabbats

The Sabbats are known as the days of the sun and earth. The Sabbats are comprised of four Earth festivals and four solar holidays, namely:

1. Earth Festivals occurring in February, May, August, and October

2. Two solstices

3. Two equinoxes

The first set of holidays or Sabbats are the days when the solar points in the calendar cross each other. For example, Wiccans celebrate Beltane on May 1, and this Sabbat falls between the Summer Solstice and Spring Equinox.

There are four holidays, namely Imbolc, Beltane, Lammas, and Samhain, that fall on days when the quarters cross. These are inspired by traditional or folk festivals that were celebrated before people adopted Christianity in Western Europe. The names of these festivals go by different names depending on the type or form of Wicca that people want to follow. Wiccans who follow Celtic traditions call Lammas as Lughnasa.

Some Wiccan traditions refer to Earth days as Greater Sabbats and cross-quarter or solar holidays as Lesser Sabbats since the former days are filled with great energy. They do this only to help Wiccans differentiate between the types of Sabbats, but it does not mean the solar days are not as important.

How did the Wheel Come into Existence?

It is important to note that Wiccans are not the only ones who follow the eight holidays since numerous Pagan traditions also follow these holidays. Some of these traditions may observe all or only some of the Sabbats. The Wiccan version of the Sabbats is unique since there is a metaphorical myth surrounding the Goddess and God. According to Wiccan texts, God and Goddess are responsible for creating nature. Each of these deities plays a divine and crucial role in the yearly cycles of animal and plant life.

According to Wiccans, God and Goddess represent the Sun and Earth, respectively, and one can view the relationship between the two in the following ways:

1. Mother and child

2. Procreating lovers

Wiccans use the absence and presence of sunlight and warmth across different seasons to understand the Wheel. The story goes as follows: God is born and grows up. Once he reaches his height of power, he does great things before he begins to age. When he nears his end, he fades away and dies before he is reborn as another being. The cycle continues every year. The Goddess is the Earth and is both the mother and creative partner to God. She is always present even when there is no light and warmth. Since the Earth is a constant in the cycle, any festival that symbolizes or worships the Earth is said to have greater power. This cycle depicts the balance between the male and female energies in the Universe, and every Sabbat is used to represent the particular stage in the life cycle.

The High Points in the Calendar

What do you think happens during a Sabbat ritual? The details of the celebration can vary, like every other element in Wicca. Generally speaking, the ritual focuses on some elements that represent the relationship shared by the two deities, and the Sabbat itself. For example, Summer and Spring Sabbats always take the theme of abundance and fertility, while the Autumn Sabbats are associated with reproduction or harvesting.

Most Wiccans always complete the Sabbat ritual, followed by a feast. These proceedings can either be elaborate or simple, and some of these rituals may involve only one practitioner, an informal Wiccan gathering, coven, or circle. Some circles and covens also hold their rituals publicly, so other members may always come and join them. People do not have to be a part of the celebration. Others may choose to perform this celebration in secrecy or celebrate in private.

The details about the ritual, including the food and decorations, are dependent on the Sabbat. Some witches may choose to devote specific parts of their rituals to some aspects of the deities at various times or points during the Wheel of the Year. They may also leave some appropriate offerings on every season and also decorate or add some objects to the altar to create seasonal themes. Some of the common names for each Sabbat used on the Calendar are listed below. The dates when these Sabbats are observed also are mentioned below:

Sabbat	Date
Yule / Winter Solstice	December 20-23*
Imbolc	February 1-2*
Ostara / Spring Equinox	March 19-21*
Beltane	April 30-May 1*
Litha / Summer Solstice	June 20-22*
Lammas	August 1-2*

Mabon / Autumn Equinox	September 21-24*
Samhain	October 31-November 1*

Both the solstices and equinoxes may fall on different dates in some parts of the world since these events occur at specific moments. Thus the day they fall on may also vary from one year to the next, and therefore, there are numerous dates for when people can maintain the Solar holidays or Sabbats.

You must practice the wheel of the year if you want to understand it fully. You should celebrate every Sabbat even if you only do something simple. After a few weeks or months, you get the hang of it, and soon you can attune your thoughts to the energy of every Sabbat. You must bear in mind that any Wiccan practice is not limited only to the Wheel of the Year since Wiccans also celebrate 13 lunar cycles every year when they perform the Esbat rituals.

The Extended Wheel of the Year

It is easy to customize the wheel for yourself by adding extra holidays that speak to your energy. Some examples are given below:

Valentine's Day/Lupercalia

This holiday is observed on February 14. Lupercalia is a Roman ancestor, and Valentine's Day is celebrated in his honor. You can celebrate this holiday by performing a ritual even though this is not an official Sabbat. You can make this a day where you celebrate love in all forms. The ritual must go beyond roses and chocolate, and you can maybe practice sex magic.

Birthday

Your birthday is special for you. Since you do not share your birthday with anybody, you know, unless you are a twin, it is your day of power. This day is the perfect time to celebrate yourself and connect with your inner or higher self.

Earth Day

Since Wiccans have a special connection to the earth, on Earth Day, you must spend some time to take care of the environment around you. For example, you can cast a spell to heal the environment around you.

Fathers' Day and Mothers' Day

Since the family is important for most people, you can integrate these days into your personal Wheel of the Year. You can celebrate fatherhood and motherhood and hold rituals to help you celebrate your loved ones.

The Bottom-Line

The Wheel of the Year may seem extremely simple, but when you dig deeper, you learn there is more to the wheel. It is not only a simple calendar. As mentioned earlier, you must practice this wheel if you want to understand it. With time, you learn to find your meaning with the different Sabbats. If you are new to this religion, it may be difficult to follow the wheel since the rituals may overwhelm you. Instead, celebrate the wheel only by performing simple rituals. When you understand each Sabbat, it becomes natural to you, and it becomes easier for you to follow the Wheel of the Year. Regardless of where you are in your journey, you must remember to know which Sabbat you want to celebrate and why.

Rites of Passage

This section sheds some light on the different rites of passage every Wiccan follower goes through.

Initiation

When someone begins to study the craft or joins a coven, they must complete their initiation ritual. When they do this, British Traditional Wiccans can always trace their lineage during the initiation ritual back to Gerald Gardner. They can then trace their lineage back from Gerald to the New Forest coven. Gardner also believed there is a traditional length to every year. When people begin to study the craft, they should go through an initiation ceremony. However, Gardner did break the rules quite often when he practiced the craft.

In Britain, traditional Wicca practices only accept someone into the first degree of Wicca. If they want to proceed to the second degree, they must go through a ceremony where they must name and describe every tool they use during rituals, and how they implement these tools. The practitioners are given their craft names during this ritual, and when they hold the second degree, they can initiate others into the craft. They can also start their own covens, but these are only semi-autonomous.

The third degree is the highest honor in British Wicca, and for one to move to this degree, they must participate in the Great rite and ritual flagellation. They can perform the great rite either symbolically or actually, depending on their feelings about the rite. When someone holds this degree, he can create autonomous covens of any parent coven.

Robert Cochrane developed the Cochranian tradition, and this Wiccan practice does not have varying degrees of initiation. It, however, has various stages that depict whether an individual is a novice or not. Some Wiccans also self-initiate themselves if they want to dedicate their lives to practice Wicca.

Handfasting

Wiccans also hold this celebration, which is similar to a Christian wedding. Some Wiccan traditions also allow couples to try staying married for a year and one day. These traditions state that the marriage must begin on Lammas and end a year and day after Lammas. They follow this since this was a traditional time for trial marriages in Ireland. One of the common vows in Wicca is "for as long as love lasts." Wiccans do not use the traditional vow, "till death do us part" when they get married. The first-ever Wiccan wedding was between Frederic Lamind and Gillian, his first wife. Their marriage took place in 1960 when they were a part of the Bricket Wood coven.

Wiccaning

Most Wiccan families perform the Wiccaning ritual, which involves babies, and this is synonymous with Christening. The objective of this rite is to present the baby to the Goddess and God to ask for their protection. Since Wicca is a tradition that people can freely follow, the child does not necessarily have to follow the same path as his parents.

The Great Rite

The Great rite is often a ritual that symbolizes sexual intercourse or is ritual sexual intercourse. In the former version, the High Priest sends the ritual knife or Athame (which represents men) into a chalice or cup (which represents women). This chalice is filled with red wine and is held by the

High Priestess. This rite symbolizes the union of the Lover God and the Maiden Goddess and is also called the fertility rite.

Numerous ritual occasions call for this rite to be performed, especially during Beltane, which occurs around November 1 in the Southern Hemisphere and May 1 in the Northern Hemisphere. This is often performed by the High Priest and Priestess, but others may also be a part of this rite.

Wicca Symbols and Signs

In Wicca, some symbols are used to represent the elements, while others are used to represent an idea. This section covers some of the commonly used symbols.

Air

Air is a classical element; it is the Element of the East, and it is invoked often in Wiccan rituals. According to Wiccan philosophies, the air is connected to the breath of life and the soul. This symbol is often associated with the colors white and yellow. In some traditions and cultures, the air is represented as a triangle, which is a masculine symbol or element. In other Wiccan traditions, the air is represented by a leaf-like image, a feather, or a circle with a point in the center. In other traditions, a triangle is not used to represent air but is used to represent the initiation rank or the association degrees that a practitioner has with the coven. This symbol is also used in alchemy, but the horizontal line extends beyond the triangle's vertices.

If you perform any rituals or cast a spell where you need to call the air element, use the triangle symbol, incense, a fan, or defender. This element is associated with wisdom, power of the mind, and communication. If you must use air, always perform the ritual on a windy day since you can harness the energy in the wind when you cast a spell. You can visualize the currents carrying away any negative energy or thoughts and carrying only positive thoughts and emotions to people who are far away. When you perform a ritual or cast a spell using air, you must embrace the wind. Let the energy fill you and intensify your intentions.

In most traditions using magic, this element is associated with different elemental beings and spirits. Sylphs, or winged creatures, are connected or associated with wind and air. These creatures represent intuition and wisdom. In some beliefs, devas and angels are also associated with air. It is important to note that a deva in new age traditions is not the same as the deva in Hinduism or Buddhism.

Celtic Shield Knot

This symbol is used both for protection and warding. Shield knots have been used in various cultures around the world and have also taken different forms. A shield knot is often represented as a square, and the design ranges from a simple to a complex knot. In the Celtic version of the symbol, a series of knots are used to represent the shield knot. In some cultures, this shield is represented as a square with loops drawn at each of the four corners.

This symbol is commonly used as a tattoo or, in some cases, as a protective talisman. Practitioners in today's Celtic groups invoke it during rituals as a way of keeping negative energy away. In some traditions, elements are represented with the knot; keep in mind that there are only three realms spiritually represented in Celtic tradition – the sea, the earth, and the sky.

While plenty of books have been written about Celtic culture and traditions, you won't find any written records detailing the existence of the Celts in the past.

The Seax Wicca

Raymond Buckland took inspiration from the Saxon religion when he founded the Seax Wicca tradition in 1973. However, you mustn't confuse the two; Seax Wicca is NOT the same as the Saxon tradition. The Seax symbol is used to represent the moon, the sun, and the eight Sabbats and was initially formed as a way of filling Buckland's own religious requirements.

In 1974, Buckland released a book entitled "The Complete Book of Saxon Witchcraft," providing guidance on the tradition. It is interesting to note that, unlike many other Wiccan religions, Seax does not require followers to take an oath of secrecy. Buckland wanted to ensure a more open and democratic experience in an attempt to move away from what he saw as self-gratifying and egotistic traditions. Most covens will elect a high priest or high priestess, and the coven, as a whole, decides when, how, and what to worship. They also allow non-members to come to some rituals, as long as the entire coven is in agreement.

The Sun Wheel

This represents the eight Sabbats that Wiccan traditionalists follow on the Wheel of the Year. The term comes from "solar cross," a calendar used in Europe for the solstices and equinoxes before Christianity was more widely adopted. There are three ways to depict the sun wheel – a circle, a cross with a wheel, and a circle and a dot.

The sun has long been a symbol representing magic and power, and, because of that, the Greeks showed prudence and piety when they honored God. Rather than wine, many Greeks preferred to give an offering of honey to the sun, believing that it was bad for the sun to become intoxicated. Because they believed that the sun was all-powerful, intoxication would lead to the sun's heat and energy destroying all life.

Something similar was used by the Egyptians, differentiating the God of Light from all the other deities by drawing the symbol above him. Invoking the sun during a ritual involved visualizing light to the east. Most of the time, this tradition is celebrated on the Midsummer Solstice and the Return at Yule Festival.

The Triple Moon

Often called the "triple goddess," this symbol is representative of the three moon phases – full moon, waxing, and waning. It has also been said, although this is somewhat questionable, that the symbol represents the three womanhood phases – maiden, mother, and crone.

The triple moon symbol represents the goddess in many traditions, including Wicca. The three crescents represent:

- The first crescent – the waxing moon, associated with new beginnings, new life, rejuvenation.

- The second crescent – the full moon, associated with the highest potency of magic, the recommended time for casting the strongest spells.

- The third crescent – the waning moon, the best time for banishing magic to be performed. This design is commonly seen in pieces of jewelry.

The Triquetra

Much like the triskele, the triquetra is a series of three overlapping arcs in a kind of triangular pattern. It is typically seen in Ireland representing the Holy Trinity, but it's fair to say that it's a much older symbol than many of the Christian traditions. It is thought to date back to around 500 BC, one of the oldest symbols, when it was used as a symbol for the triple goddess. It is known in some traditions as the Rune of Protection and symbolizes Earth, Air, and Water.

Today, thy symbol is popular in jewelry, knotwork, emblems, and so on, where a tri-fold symbol is needed – life, death, and rebirth, love, honor, protect, and so on. Often, a circle is interlaced into the triquetra, indicating the bond that ties the elements.

This symbol is referred to as a Celtic symbol but is also used in various Nordic traditions. Historians have found this symbol on Germanic coins and on runestones in Sweden. There is a strong similarity between this symbol and the valknut design used in the Norse traditions, and the latter represents Odin. This symbol has been found in various Celtic artworks and in the Book of Kells. It often appears in jewelry and metalwork. This symbol never appears by itself, and historians and researchers speculate that this symbol was first created to only use as a filler to fill up a blank space.

This symbol may also appear within a circle and is also represented as a circle that has three overlapping sections. Most Wiccans use this symbol as a power of three. They believe this symbol represents the magical abilities of three witches, and they derived this belief from the Television Series Charmed.

Water

Water is one of the four classical elements, and this is feminine energy. It is connected closely with the goddess. In some Wiccan traditions, especially the British coven, water is used to represent the second degree of initiation. The inverted triangle is used to represent water, and this is a feminine symbol. This symbol is closely associated with the shape of the womb. Some traditions also represent water as horizontal crossbars within a circle or a series of wavy lines.

Since water is connected to the West, it is related to purification and healing. Western traditions use holy water, which is regular water with salt, in any spiritual ritual or path. Salt is another symbol of purification. In most covens, saltwater is always used to protect the circle and the objects or symbols placed on the altar.

Most traditions and cultures use water spirits in their mythology and folklore. In Greek mythology, a water spirit, known as a naiad, presides over a stream or spring. Romans also had a similar entity in their religion. If you want to practice divination, you can use water for scrying at the time of the full moon. Ellen Dugan, the author of elements of witchcraft, suggested that it is best to meditate if you want to communicate with water spirits. It is also best to use waters in various rituals that involve fluid emotions, like love. Some practitioners prefer to cast a spell near a stream or river. You should let the current carry away any negative emotions or thoughts you want to be rid of.

Yin Yang

This symbol represents spirituality and is more influenced by Eastern cultures than contemporary Wicca or Pagan. This symbol does require some mentioning since you can find it across the world, and this is one symbol most people recognize.

This symbol represents the polarity of every being in the universe and is often used to represent balance. Black and white are the equal portions of the symbol, and each is surrounded by a circle of the opposing color. This shows there is balance in the various forces in the universe. This symbol represents the balance between dark and light or a link between two opposite forces.

Some cultures place the white portion on top while others place it at the bottom. The symbol finds its origins in Chinese symbols, but it is also used in Buddhism to represent the rebirth cycle. This symbol is also used in Taoism and symbolizes the Tao itself. It is also known as Taiji.

The Yin Yang symbol is traditionally Asian, but many similar images have been found across the globe. Some Roman centurions have also used this symbol. That said, there is no evidence to connect the images from the Roman Empire to those found in the eastern world.

It is best to use this symbol if you want to perform rituals where you must call for harmony or balance. If you want polarity in your life, use this symbol as your guide. You can also use this symbol if you are on a quest for spiritual rebirth. In some traditions, this symbol is described as the valley and a mountain. As the sun climbs over the mountain, the valley is illuminated because of the sunlight. When the sun faces the opposite side, the mountain loses light, and so does the valley. Visualize the shift in sunlight when you use the symbol to cast a spell.

Chapter Three: Types of Magic

White Magic

Most practitioners divide magic into two types – white magic and black magic. The former is also known as the right-hand path, while the latter is known as the left-hand path. The definition of these forms of magic is often debated, but the one commonly accepted is that white magic is associated with healing and positivity, while black magic only represents harm and negativity. Some also believe that white magic is used for a good while black magic is always done to appease the spell caster. Regardless, the actual practice of both forms of magic is dependent on the belief system, individual practitioners, and schools of thought.

Setting up the Altar

Pick the Base

You can position your altar on a flat surface or raised surface. Ensure the altar is wide enough to accommodate your ritual items and your Book of Shadows. You can use a nightstand, coffee table, large storage chest, or a shelf. Some practitioners prefer to use a round altar since it is easy for them to move around the table when they cast their spells. Others prefer rectangular or square altars since it is easy to store the items. It is recommended that you choose an altar made of wood or any other material found in nature.

Identify the Spot

You must always pick the spot where it is generally quiet since you need to concentrate when you cast a spell. Some Wiccan traditions state that the altar must always be placed facing either the East or North, but the direction depends on the school of thought. Always place the altar in a spot where there is natural light. You can place the altar in a spot you believe is positive or associated with creation.

Arrange the Symbols

When you set up the altar, you must place the necessary symbols around the altar. These symbols help to centralize the energy in the objects. The items you use can represent Mother Goddess or the Horned God. You can also use personal deities of your choice. Some practitioners choose to use different colored candles to represent the elements of deities, while others purchase figures to represent them. Some practitioners, however, pick items that give meaning to their beliefs, and these items are derived from traditions and myths.

Represent the Elements

Most traditions use different symbols to represent the four elements, and these symbols are arranged around the altar. Place the symbols as per their cardinal directions. When you perform white magic, you should use light or white colored items to represent the elements.

Casting Spells

Always Determine Your Intent

Make sure to have a clear goal in mind when you always cast a spell or perform a ritual. Always remember that white magic is positive, and it does not harm anybody. This form of magic encourages happiness, growth, peace, healing, etc. Most people believe that white magic does not give the spell caster power over the other person. When you follow this tenet, you must never cast a love spell where you force someone to fall for you or love you. Instead, use the white magic to attract an unknown person instead of using the spell to force someone to fall in love with you. Some of the spells in the fifth chapter in this book ask you only to visualize the ideal partner for you and then cast the spell.

Select Objects to Enhance Your Spell

You can use different objects to cast your spell. You can use different items that are personal to you or have some meaning. Always draw from your covens or cultural symbols and traditions when you cast a spell. You can also use specific figurines and herbs to strengthen your spell. Do not overcrowd your altar when you perform a spell. When you cast a white magic love spell, you must represent the qualities you look for in a partner around your altar. You can add a dash of spice or pepper to the altar if you want someone who is passionate. Represent intelligence using the statue of an owl. You can also use saffron to represent an individual who is stable or happy.

Cast Your Protective Circle

As mentioned in the first chapter, you must create a protective circle around yourself when you cast a spell. Create this circle around the altar and stand in the center before you cast a spell. You can use a string, stones, salt, twigs, chalk, or other objects to draw the circle. Cast your spell by facing the altar.

Meditate

The objects you put on your altar can be used in meditation, as a way of clearing your mind of negativity. Meditation is the best way to ensure you can focus on your intent when casting spells. Your energy can be channeled using a wand or knife, and your focus should be on a certain object on the altar. Try to relate every object to the spell you are casting and say a prayer, calling on the deities or elements to help you.

Use the Right Words

Spell-casting and rituals require you to use the right words in your incantations. There's no need to use an actual spell every time; just pick the words that match your intent. If you want to use spells, do plenty of research before you start, or approach an experienced practitioner for help. Once you have some experience, you can start writing your own spells, transcribing them into your own Book of Shadows.

Whatever spell you intend to cast, memorize it first. If you have to keep stopping to read the words, it won't work. Also, be careful never to perform a spell or ritual that could result in violence, use any negative phrases, or hateful words.

Red Magic

We've all heard of black magic and white magic, but what about red magic? It does exist and is often referred to as "sex" magic. A late Roman exorcist, Gabriele Amorth, published a book titled "An Exorcist Explains the Demonic," describing red magic as "sorcery that influences sentiment and the sphere of sexuality."

Termed as "hoodoo" in some American and African cultures, red magic actually has a much simpler explanation. It is the most basic magic used in many practicing communities, enlightening practitioners to the fact that all of us have magic within us; our bodies are merely the vessel, the medium with which we communicate with the so-called 'real world.'

The reason red magic became known as sex magic was that, typically, two people would cast the spells. These would have been lovers, or two people married to one another. The spells were usually cast to join their minds, bodies, and spirits by giving their souls to one another. This could only be done through sex, which is how red magic got its reputation as sex magic. However, it should be borne in mind that this is not strictly true as the two people did not have to be lovers; they could be friends or acquaintances of the same or opposite sex. The only requirement was that the two people were connected spiritually.

The 'hoodoo' term was derived from what is considered the most powerful magic on earth, voodoo. This was practiced by Africans who were taken, as slaves, to America, a place that knew little about voodoo, only that it was a type of religion practiced by these people. Red magic was seen as being much the same as voodoo, simply because of the ritual sacrifices and offerings made before a spell was cast.

Right now, there is little information recorded about red magic, but the belief is that it started back in medieval times.

Black Magic

Black magic has always been seen as the evil magic, dark magic used for purely selfish or evil reasons, You can see white and black magic as two sides to a path, with the black magic being on the left, dark and malevolent, while the white magic shines on the right side of the path.

Black magic can be traced thousands of years back, as can white magic. Where we can draw parallels between white magic and shamanism, in that both attempted to become close to spiritual beings, black magic was used to invoke the same spirits but for the selfish benefit of the person performing the ritual. These days, black magic is still associated with that and also with evil, with many people believing it is used only to harm others, to bring about their destruction.

Black magic isn't just about intent, though. It's about the tools you use to perform it. They tend to be hot, pointed, and caustic. Practitioners use personal things from their intended victim, such as blood, or hair, and black magic spells are typically cast at night. Practitioners may also ask an underworld demon to help them.

Voodoo has long been associated with black magic, but much of this comes down to movies and books that aren't factually correct. In fact, voodoo has a history all of its own, traditions that have very little association with modern magic and witchcraft. However, because of their use of magic associated with poison, zombies, and curses, voodooists now have an unenviable association with black magic.

Protection Against Black Magic

If you fear being targeted by black magic, there are several protective objectives you can use. These include certain crystals and spells you can cast against negative energy. We'll look more at these later.

Chapter Four: The Book of Shadows

A book of shadows is the book you write your spells and rituals in. That's the simple explanation, but there is a bit more to it. It's your guidebook, as it were, a book containing the basic practices, philosophy, rituals, and Wiccan ethics, as well as your own personal rituals and spells. In some Wiccan traditions, the Book of Shadows passes from one coven member to another, and the high priest or priestess will handwrite rituals and spells, copying them from the initiating witch. If you are initiated into a coven, you will then copy those spells and rituals, from the high priest or priestess's book into yours. You, and you alone, are responsible for maintaining your Book of Shadows.

But where did the Book of Shadows start? A Wiccan by the name of Gerald Gardener claims he created the first book, around the 1940s to 1950s, using it in the Bricket Wood Coven he created. He claims to have said to the coven that the Book was his own book of spells and rituals that he found had worked and offered to let others cop or change them as they saw fit.

But Gardner didn't work alone, enlisting the help of Doreen Valiente, a high-priestess. Over the years, many attempts have been made to keep this original Book of Shadows a secret, but, over the years, it has been republished several times under different names.

The Rewriting

In 1953, Valiente joined the coven at Bricket Lane, and it didn't take long before she became the high priestess. Gardner had originally claimed that the material in his Book of Shadows had come from ancient sources. Still, it didn't take Valiente long to realize that much of it had come from more recent sources, such as "The Gospel of the Witches," "Key of Solomon," and from famed occultist, Aleister Crowley, among other places. When

Valiente talked to Gardner about this, he admitted it and told her to rewrite the book herself if she thought she could do a better job. She took him up on that challenge, removing anything that came from or was related to Crowley, given the negativity surrounding his reputation, and writing it as she thought it should be.

British Traditional Wicca

In some forms of British Traditional Wicca, the book of shadows is used by those practitioners who adhere to the Wiccan Rede. British Traditional Wicca includes the following covens – Gardnerian Wicca, Algard Wicca, and Alexandrian Wicca. Practitioners use the book written by Valiente and Gardner. Gardner wrote his book along with Doreen Valiente, and this book included information from numerous modern sources. This book also included various sections written in different styles and included information about witches who were tortured and killed for performing witchcraft. Gardner claimed these sections were historical, and witches were never allowed to write in their book of shadows only until the late early 1900s when people began to accept the uses of magic. He believed that was the reason why most witches avoided writing in their book. When people accepted the use of the book of shadows, many witches began to write various rituals and spells in their personal books. They, however, jumbled the order of the rituals and steps to prevent any novice from using them. Scholars and researchers, however, doubt the authenticity of this information.

According to research, Gardner told his subsequent followers to copy the book word for word. He also told people that Wiccans descended from Monique Wilson, Eleanor Bone, and Patricia Crowther.

Contemporary Usage

Some traditional practitioners maintained two books of shadow. The first book is used to maintain the core rituals that do not change. The second book is used for rituals used by the coven. An initiate, someone who just joined the coven, was allowed to copy rituals from either book. The second book is maintained only by the coven with rituals and practices that the coven must follow. This book differs from one group to the next, but covens do share some information with each other. Some practitioners also maintain a personal book of shadows in addition to the other books. They use this book for personal use and do not pass it on to anybody else.

Publication

After Gardner passed away, Charles Cardell, his rival, published most of the material he found in the book of shadows written by Gardner. Stewart Farrar and Janet Farrar, who were Alexandrians, decided to publish the Gardnerian book in its true form. They obtained Doreen Valient's permission before they published the book in 1984. This book was titled 'The Witches' Way.'

Non-Traditional Wicca

Eclectic or nontraditional forms of Wicca or other neo-Pagan practices, practitioners use the book of shadows to describe a personal Journal. According to these traditions, the witch describes or journals various rituals, spells, and the results of those rituals and spells. They do not pass this book from teacher to student. Now, the book of shadows is maintained electronically. It is not always a handwritten book. Some witches or practitioners still use the book of shadows to record various spells, but they call it the book of mirrors since it contains their experiences, thoughts, and feelings.

Representation in Popular Culture

Charmed, a television fantasy series, features the book of shadows. According to this television show, this book contains arcane law and various spells. It also has the ability to defend itself from any negative energy or harm. The craft, a 1996 film, was a major influence on the charming television series. In this movie, the book was referred to as a diary maintained by the witch. The witch always wrote down power thoughts in this book.

The sequel of the Blair witch project was titled book of shadows. There was, however, a new mention of this book during the film. Critics believe that the title was used as an attempt to capitalize on the established audience of the charming TV series.

What You Should and Shouldn't Write in Your Book

As a Wiccan, you will have many different supplies, but the most important is your Book of Shadows. No coven member will have the exact same spells, rituals, or other information in their book because it is an intensely personal item. And that is also why your Book of Shadows should be kept hidden from all other eyes but your own.

What all this means is that you can pretty much write what you want in your Book, but I will give you some ideas on what should and shouldn't be in there. Trust me when I say that, later down the line, you will find your Book fulfilling if you put the right things in it and leave the wrong things out.

What Should Be in There

Your Name

This goes without saying, really; as the book is yours, make sure you own it with your name.

Your Wiccan Tradition

You should include your beliefs, the path you follow, and what sort of Wiccan you are.

The Wiccan Rede

This binds all Wiccan traditions together. Most religions are full of commandments and laws, but Wiccans bow to just two – the Threefold law, which says that whatever you do in life comes back to you three times over and the Wiccan Rede, which says, "An it harm none, do as ye will."

Your Personal Deities

The deities you choose are personal, particularly when you practice alone, and you must choose the ones that you have a connection with, that you truly believe in. Write the name of the deity in your Book, the name of their pantheon, what meaning they have for you, and any other information.

Your Rituals and Spells

These are all the rituals you like to do, those that you have created by yourself, and the ones that you want to try in the future. Do the same for the spells – all the ones you tried and loved, those you created and those you want to try. When you write each one, include as much information as you can, such as the recipes so you can have everything ready when you next perform it.

The Sabbats and Rituals

Write each Sabbat down and write what the seasons mean for you. List the rituals you like to do during the Sabbats you listed and state how your altar is decorated for each particular Sabbat.

Specific Correspondence Charts

This includes your crystal chart, herbal correspondence chart, and your candle color chart. Your Book of Shadows is much like a reference book and, having all the important stuff written in one place means you don't need to keep piles of books that will end up being thrown away at some point.

Your Thoughts, Your Reflections, and Your Experiences

You should also consider your Book of Shadows as a kind of diary or a journal, and you should write down everything relevant along your spiritual journey. When you look back over it, you can see your mindset at any given time, your realizations, and so on, Don't be shy about what you write; it is for your eyes only.

Your other Wiccan supplies, such as altar patens, smudge bowls, candles, etc., can be replaced, but your Book of Shadows cannot. You have no chance of rewriting it all as it was, and you can't relive the experiences you had in the past.

What Shouldn't Be in Your Book

While there are things that definitely should be in your Book of Shadows, by the same token, there are things that should not.

The idea of your Book is to record your journey, both spiritual and magickal. It is a Book you can look back on in years to come, and you don't want to read anything negative, or you don't want your daughters to read anything negative when you pass it onto them.

What you shouldn't include in your book are:

Things That Are Not Connected With Magick or Wicca

This is your personal account of your own spiritual Wiccan journey, not your household chores list, grocery list, or a place to sort out your household bills. It is for you to write you rituals, spells, thoughts, dreams, etc., that are all related to Wicca.

Hate-Filled Thoughts

Lots of people are tempted to write things down in the heat of the moment, bad thoughts they may have about a partner or someone else. Yes, this is a great way to let off some steam, but keep those thoughts out of your Book of Shadows. You can always start a separate journal for that sort of thing if it makes you feel better. You will only regret it later down the line when you look through your Book and find it filled with hatred and negative thoughts. At the end of the day, negativity can fade out of your life; writing it in your Book of Shadows only keeps it alive forever.

Hexes and Curses

Wicca is white, not black magick; it's about purity and shining lights. Wicca is a peaceful religion, based on a lover of nature and very grounded. It isn't about black curses and hexes, and it isn't about abandoning the Divine. Don't forget the threefold law and the Wiccan Rede; if you start dabbling in curses, you won't be on the right side of the Divine.

Entries From Someone Else

What that means, of course, is that you shouldn't allow anyone else to write their entries in your Book of Shadows. Keep your own Book, and keep it just for you. Don't even let anyone else read it, let alone write in it. If a friend has thoughts of their own that they want to write down, tell them to get a Book of their own, and don't give in to pressure.

As you can see, there is much you can write in your book and little that you shouldn't. Stick to these guidelines and your Book of Shadows will be perfect for you. You will be able to go back through it in the years to come, see how far you progressed, how much you achieved along the way. And when you pass it on to your daughter or your granddaughter, you are passing on a Book you are proud of.

Chapter Five: Love and Relationship Spells

I am not too sure what you may have in your kitchen cupboard at the moment, so this chapter has some simple love spells you can use. You will definitely have the ingredients needed to cast these spells.

Red Candle Spell

To perform this spell, you need the following:

- Red yarn or ribbon

- Two Red taper candles

- Candle dressing

- Sharp knife or carving tool

Follow the steps given below to cast this spell:

- The first step is to dress the candles. Write or carve your name and your partner's name on separate candles. You can also carve a desired outcome or petition to perform this spell. Cleanse the candles and then dress them however you want to purify them. Now, set your intention for the spell on the candles

● The next step is to bind the candles, and you can do this using the ribbon or yarn. You can tie seven knots, but always choose a number you resonate with. Set the intention while you tie the knots. It can be as simple as, "With this knot, I bind us together in love."

● The last step is to light the candles, and, as you are now bound together, you must bring your intention into the spell. Let the candles burn until they go out naturally, or the candle melts fully. You can dress the altar or plate with candles with different love items, such as sugar, honey, rose petals, etc. You can also use tarot cards when these candles burn.

Ribbon Spell

To cast this spell, you need the following:

- Red or pink ribbon

- Pepper and saltshakers, or any other objects that make a pair, such as your favorite shoes, a set of bookends, etc.

Follow the steps given below to cast this spell:

- Wait for the New Moon to conduct this spell.

- Pick the objects. It is important to note that one of the objects represents you, while the other represents your partner.

- Now, take the ribbon and bind the two together and leave some space between the two.

- Untie the ribbon every morning, and move the objects closer to each other and retie the knot.

- Do this until the objects touch each other.

- Now, leave the shoes tied together for a few more days or until you meet your new love.

Rose Spell

To cast this spell, you will need the following:

● A source of moving water, preferably a river, ocean or stream, but if you do not live close to any water body, use the washbasin or bathtub

● Rose Petals

To cast this spell, follow the steps given below:

● The first thing you must do is to visualize the person whom you desire to be your lover or partner.

● Now, collect the petals of a rose and throw them to the water while you chant the following: "As this rose flows out to waters so that true love will find me."

● Repeat this process twice and make sure to visualize your dream lover.

● Always throw the petals so that the water brings them back to you to ensure the Universe knows you need love to come to you.

Fairy Love Spell

When you want to draw new love, you should start planting red primroses in your garden. So, go to the local nursery and buy a few red primroses. Pot them and place them either near your front or backdoor. Every night touch the pot with both hands and gaze at the plants. Focus all your energy on the flowers and say the following:

"Flower of love, realm of the fey,

Bring me a lover before it is May."

Repeat the spell every Friday until you find your true love. When this happens, thank the flower and place a shiny dime in the pot. Then snip one blossom from the pot and slip that into a muslin bag. Leave the bag near your clothes and pin it close to your heart when you get dressed for work or go out. When you do this, observe the feelings associated with love and feel them deeply. Visualize the love you want to attract. When you tend to the flowers regularly and devote yourself to keeping the plant alive, you will soon find your true love. When your spell succeeds, share a drink with your partner and offer the first glass to the flower.

Love Poppet

A love or spell poppet uses the principles of sympathetic magic. Sympathetic magic is a form of magic based on the idea that when you perform an action on any object, that action affects everything that the object represents. These poppets are often referred to as Voodoo dolls, but they are not bad objects to use. The term is a misnomer since Voodoo represents a set of religious traditions followed in West Africa, and this culture is prevalent in Caribbean and Louisiana populations. Voodoo dolls do not have too much prominence in either of these traditions, but they appear in numbers of magical traditions across the globe.

The Western culture, unfortunately, demonizes voodoo dolls and taints the beautiful, complex, and rich traditions of voodoo itself. It is for these reasons we use the term poppet to represent this doll. This doll is not used to torture the target, and you do not have to poke it with needles. It is used to draw money, power, luck, and love. For this spell, you must create a poppet that represents the person you love.

Tips for This Spell Poppet Tutorial

It is easy to make your poppet, and if you know how to thread the needle and use scissors, you are sorted. There are some issues you must note when it comes to stitching. Do not fear, because this section will help you prevent any mistakes that people often make.

1. Do not try to keep the stitches inside the poppet, since that will not work. If you want to stitch inside the poppet, you need a very large poppet.

2. Use the whip stitch

Do not panic if you do not know these stitches. They are extremely easy to learn.

Choosing a Fabric

It is best to work with cotton quilting fabric since it is easy to stitch them. You can customize the spell any way you need, depending on what you want from life. For this spell, let us choose a rose print since roses represent romance, love, and attraction. The mileage you choose may vary, but it would be best to choose a cool blue fabric if you want a healing poppet and a green one to attract wealth or money. You can do as you please.

To do this, you need the following:

- Love herbs like lavender, rosemary and dried roses

- Sturdy scrap paper or cardstock. You can also use cardboard or cereal boxes

- 1/8 yard quilting fabric, preferably cotton

- Matching thread

- Scissors

Follow the steps given below to make your poppet:

Step 1

Fold the cardstock and draw the outline of the shape of the goddess. You can use any shape you like to depict the goddess.

Step 2

Cut the shape of your choice and open it. Place it directly on the fabric you want to use and cut two pieces of fabric using that shape.

Step 3

Now, place the incorrect sides of the poppet together, but do not sew it yet. Turn the sides out unless you want to make a large poppet. You can use a basic whipstitch around the edges, but leave an opening at the bottom of the poppet.

Step 4

Now, add a little fiber or cotton to the poppet to fill it. Do this only if you want it to be plush. Do not add stones or cotton since that will not help you during the spell. You can use a combination of the following herbs:

- Lavender

- Rosemary

- Orange peel

- Dried apple peel

- Dried roses

Now, sew the opening of the poppet.

Step 5

You are finally ready to charge the poppet. Let us first do some quick clearing of energy from the poppet. You can do any of the steps mentioned below to charge the poppet with energy:

- Leave the poppet near your window and let it bask in the moonlight

- Sleep with the poppet close to your pillow for at least seven nights

- Make a circle with candles and place the poppet in between the candles for a few hours

You can also use any other method you like to charge the poppet

Kiss the Moonlight - A Strong Love Charm

The moon is incredibly powerful, as it the light that shines from it, especially when you want to perform magic. That power works well for any love spells, including this one.

You will need

- Red or pink rose petals

- Piece of rose quartz

- A small bowl of silver

You must perform this ritual at night, preferably on the day of the new moon. This means you cannot view the moon at night. Kiss the crystal and put it into the bowl. Now sprinkle the rose petals over the stone and place the bowl close to the window. Leave the bowl near the window for seven days. Once seven days have passed, pick up the crystal and use it, drawing romance and love to you. The bowl can now be placed near to the window, with the petals in it, until another full moon arrives.

Love Star

The Love Star spell must be cast on a clear night when all the stars are out. Gather the ingredients listed below and position yourself close to a wide-open window so that you can see the stars:

You will need:

- A red candle
- Jasmine incense stick
- Pink or red crystals, like Carnelian, Garnet, or a Rose Quartz

Place the candle and the incense stick on your altar and light both of them. Focus on the brightest star you can see in the sky and gather the crystals into your hands. Close your eyes, visualize the light from that bright star filling the crystals and say the following words, three times:

Star of love, burn so bright   Aid me in my spell tonight   Unite my true love to me   As I will it, so mote it be.

After the third incantation, put the crystals onto your altar, close to your candle, and leave the candle and incense to burn out by themselves.

As Friday's ruler is the goddess of love, Venus, these spells should be cast on that day. You can be particular about your timing if you want to be, and wait for the crescent or new moon to cast the spells. During those moons, the energy is positive, creative, and it helps in attracting newness to you.

A Love Pouch With a Magnetic Lodestone

This is the absolute best stone for this purpose as magnetic lodestones are known for symbolizing attraction. Use natural lodestones where you can, but if you cannot find them, you can use small magnets to cast this spell. You also need:

- `Love drawing oil`

- `1 small red bag`

You can either use a purchased blend of oils designed for love spells or make your own oil. Use a mixture of ylang-ylang, rose, cardamom, ginger, and vanilla oils to create a potent love blend. Add a few drops to your palm and rub them. Now, rub the lodestones to anoint them with the loving blend. Continue to rub the stones until your palms are warm. Now, concentrate on the stones and draw romance and love into your life. Drop the stones into the bag and continue to rub the bag in your hands. Let some of the oil stick to the bag as well. Now, place this bag near your bedside table or in your bag to attract your true love.

Chapter Six: Money and Wealth Rituals

Now that we have looked at the various spells and rituals to bring love into your life, let us look at some rituals to help you bring in more wealth and money.

Rice Ritual

You should only perform this ritual when you know nobody is going to visit your home. If you want, you can ask for the Archangel Uriel to help you when you perform this spell, so nobody interrupts your ritual. When you perform this ritual with a strong belief and intent, you will see the results sooner than expected.

To perform this ritual, you need the following ingredients:

- Rice

- Two glass jars with lids

- Six grains of black pepper

- Two green candles

To perform the ritual, follow the steps given below:

- Place the jars and lids in boiling water to sterilize them, and then dry them properly.

- Place a handful of rice in both jars and add three gains of pepper above the rice. Now, seal the jars.

- Place one jar in the dining room and the other in the kitchen. If you do not have a separate dining room, you can place both on opposite sides of the kitchen. Make sure you place the jars in an area that is easily visible to you.

● Place one candle in front of each jar and light it. Let the candle burn for two hours before you wave them out.

● Discard the candles and leave the jars in the same area for the next time you perform this ritual.

An Abundance of Money Ritual

Using nothing more than sugar and gold coins, you can attract money to you easily. The combination of sugar and coins creates the energy required to attract money. Choose a Thursday night or the crescent moon for this ritual.

You will need:

- Three gold coins
- Some white sugar
- A wide-mouthed clear glass jar
- A smaller glass to go inside the big one
- Red ribbon

Here's how to do this ritual:

- Pour sugar into the large jar, filling it up
- Put the small glass inside the large glass and twist it to set it firmly into the sugar
- The coins go into the small jar and then the red ribbon is tied around the large jar
- As you are doing all this, say these words, over and again – "Abundance of money."
- When you have completed this, stand facing the main door to the house
- Place your glass jars just inside the door on the left-hand side. Make sure it is not where it can be kicked or knocked over when people come through the door.

Water Ritual

This ritual is designed to attract enough money to you to last the whole month and requires just two simple ingredients – a glass of water and two heaped tablespoons of table salt or sea salt.

- On the first Sunday in the month, fill up a glass with water – tap or bottled water, either will do. Add one tablespoon of salt and leave it for one hour
- Pour the salt water over your hands, washing them thoroughly. Say the words, "Salt is my protector; it will make money multiply, so my home lacks for nothing."
- Leave your hands to dry naturally, not with a towel or anything else
- Add the rest of the salt to another glass of water
- Place it in one corner of a room in your house and leave it for 24 hours – it will absorb the negative energy swirling around
- Pour the contents of the glass away after 24 hours and sit back and watch the money come to you throughout the month.

Green Candle Money Ritual

You need to perform this ritual five days before the day you are to receive the money since it takes five days to complete it. This is a great ritual that helps you manifest some money. Before you perform the ritual, you must think about the money you need and visualize that it is already in your account.

To perform this ritual, you need the following:

- Peppermint oil

- One green pillar candle

- One white sheet of paper

- One silver coin

To perform this ritual, follow the steps given below:

- Write the amount of money you need on the piece of paper.

- Smear or rub the candle with the oil using your hands

- Place the coin on one side of the candle and draw a dollar sign using the edge of the coin.

- Now, light the candle and think about the money you need, and visualize it coming into your home for at least ten minutes.

- Fold the paper with the amount you need to be written on it. Fold it thrice lengthwise and three more times to form a square. You should have an envelope in your hand.

● Place the coin inside the envelope and seal it using the wax from the candle.

● Now hold the envelope close to your chest and say the following, "Money I need come to me." Chant this spell however many times you would like to, but say it as you mean it

● Now, place the envelope under the candle holder and let the candle burn for another twenty minutes. Wave the candle out with your hand and do not blow it out

● Continue the ritual for the next five days by lighting it every morning and focusing on your intent.

Pumpkin Spice For More Cash

This ritual is one of the best ways to expand your income. You can use this if your income often depends on a bonus program or commission. The only ingredient you need to perform this ritual is one large can of pumpkin spice. Follow the steps given below to perform this ritual:

● Put some money aside five days before you are due to get paid and sprinkle it with pumpkin spice. Now, wave the wad of cash in front of the main door to your house.

- Five days or more before you are due to get paid, sprinkle your shoes with more pumpkin spice.

That is all you need to do. Now, look for any opportunities where you can get a bigger paycheck. The ingredients used to make pumpkin spice are a mix of those that attract money. If you want to make your own mix, use the spices and herbs listed below:

- Cloves
- Thyme
- Nutmeg
- Ginger
- Allspice
- Basil
- Cinnamon

Pay a Bill

Cast this spell if there is a specific debt or bill you must pay, and you are not looking only for general prosperity. To perform this spell, you need the following:

- `Cinnamon oil or patchouli`

- `Incense`

- `A piece of paper`

- `Green candle`

To cast this spell, follow the steps given below:

- `Use the pen to draw some symbols to represent the bill on the paper. You can use logos, words, dollar figures, or any other symbols that represent the bill. Since you will burn this paper, do not use a real bill. You can use a photocopy of a dollar bill to cast this spell. That said, it is best to use your own drawing as it has a kind of energy associated with it.`

- `Smear or rub the candle with the oil and place the paper under the holder. Now, light the incense and candle and repeat the following while you watch the flames:`

"The candle burns

And lights the way

For money coming

This bill will pay"

● Focus on the bill and why you must pay it off. Let the candle burn for 10 minutes while you visualize yourself paying off the bill. Burn this candle every day for seven days, so make sure the candle is large enough. Remove the candle on the seventh day and burn the paper completely. Let the candle continue to burn until it goes out.

● If you want to honor the spell, put any unexpected earnings towards this bill. Otherwise, you may end up losing the money.

Wealth Attraction Bath

You can use this bath mixture at any time during the day, but it is best to use it before you attend an event where you can earn money. So, use this mixture before a bank visit, a job interview, or a business meeting. All you need to do this are:

- 3 drops pine oil
- 3 drops cinnamon oil
- 3 drops basil oil
- A handful of sea salt
- Small bottle or vial with a tight lid
- A pinch of patchouli herb

Follow the steps given below to use this mixture:

- Run a bath, and when the water is warm, add the herb, salt, and oils to the water.
- Soak in the mixture for at least 15 minutes. While you are in the tub, think about the event and visualize how it may bring money into your life.
- Visualize the outcome you want
- Fill the bottle or vial with the bathwater and place the lid. Now, drain the bath.
- Carry the vial or bottle with you to the meeting.

Welcome Wealth Spell

If you want to welcome wealth and prosperity into your home, you can cast a welcoming spell on the main entrance to your house.

You will need

- A doormat
- Some sandalwood chips
- A small handful of dried patchouli
- A small handful of dried basil
- One silver coin

To cast your spell

- Position your doormat outside the main entrance to the house
- When you are happy with the position, lift it and spread the basil, patchouli, and sandalwood beneath it
- Bury the coin within the herbal mixture and place the mat back over the top
- Stand upon your mat and face to the north. Say the following words:

"I welcome wealth to my home.

Please stop here, do not roam.

My welcome mat is here you see

Bring in new prosperity."

Move off the mat. Now welcome wealth opportunities to start flowing in

Chapter Seven: Health and Wellbeing Spells

Energy Spells

When you are feeling low, your morale is all but gone, and you need your spirits to lift you out of the doldrums, try an energy spell. These spells let you tap into the Earth's energy and use it to boost your own. You may not be filled with boundless energy, but you will get enough of a boost so that you can get through the day on a happier note. Here are some of the more popular energy spells.

Relight the Spark

The name says it all here; you want your spirit relit and replenished, and this is the spell to do it. It is one of the simpler spells and provides just enough power to put you back in control.

You will need an orange candle, some orange yarn, a stick of cinnamon, and a heatproof pan or dish. You must have enough yarn to wrap around the candle a few times.

Hold the candle and begin wrapping the yarn around it, making equally spaced knots in it as you go – the knots must all be touching the surface of the candle.

Next, put the candle into a candle holder and prepare your mind, so you are fully focused on the spell. Block out all external distractions, go into your mind, and try to feel the energy that comes from within the earth. You should feel an energy surge, starting from your feet and traveling up your body to your head.

Once your mind and body are filled with this energy, hold it there, and light your cinnamon stick. Repeat the following, out loud, a minimum of four times – "Energy, power, rise up the tower."

Now hold the cinnamon stick to the candle and, when the candle is alight, leave it to burn for a few moments. When the flame is steady, place the candle into the heatproof pan or dish. Focus only on the energy from the fire as it begins to eat away at the wax. Do not allow your focus to become disturbed, and do not break your focus until the candle has burned down entirely.

Crystal Booster Bag

Every day is different, and you can't possibly know what each one will bring. Sometimes you will sail through a day with no trouble while, on others, you might suddenly find yourself in a panic, weighed down with a ton of work or chores that just have to be done right now. With the crystal booster, you can create a spell that you can use at the drop of a hat, a spell to help you when what was a standard steady day, suddenly turns into a hectic mess. This spell will provide you with a boost of strength, the drive you need to power through to the end of the day.

You will need a small blue or white bag made from cloth, some cedarwood chips (or you can just add a few drops of cedarwood oil to standard wood chips), and one each of the following crystals – pyrite, citrine, red jasper, and bloodstone.

There is nothing complicated about this spell; just place all of your ingredients into the cloth bag, and tie it with a tight knot. Place it in your handbag or a bag that you take to work with you every day, and it will help you face the day ahead and cope with any tough parts of the day.

Happiness Spells

You might have heard, somewhere along the way, that you can pull happiness out of nowhere with just a simple happiness spell. Sorry, but it doesn't work that way, and neither can you induce a happy state of mind. What happiness spells do is help you shed off stress, and that should make you happier.

What you must keep in mind that magic isn't a cure and, if your heart isn't in it or your mind isn't in the right place, these spells may not work or may not provide you with the result you want. Happiness spells can give you a bit of a boost if you are feeling a little low, but don't expect them to remove depression or serious, deep-hearted sorrow by themselves. Part of making any spell work, especially happiness spells, is to put the effort in to improve your mood by yourself; if you don't, these spells are unlikely to work.

The primary ingredient for any happiness spell is to ensure your mind is clear and in the right mental place.

Three Candle Joy Spell

This spell is designed to give you a burst of positivity when you are at your lowest ebb. You will need three candles – orange, yellow, or a combination of both – a couple of pinches of dried rosemary or marjoram, and cedar oil.

Apply the cedar oil to the candles and then position them on your altar, Light them in turn and sprinkle your dried herbs around them on the altar. Calm your mind, focus your attention on the heat coming from the candle flames. Stretch your hands over the heat and, when you begin to feel the fire's energy radiating towards you, channel that power, saying the following words aloud -

"Happiness and joy come into my life.

Away with anger, stress, and strife

I am happy; I am free

No more negativity."

Do make sure that you don't get your hands too close to the flame – the last thing you want is to burn them!

Blooming Happiness

A blooming spell takes energy from positive energy vibes given off by flowers. You will some lilac or jasmine oil, any fresh flower, a heatproof dish, a yellow candle, a pencil, and some paper.

Focus your mind on three things that are negatively affecting your happiness. Light your candle and write all these on the paper. Now hold the paper to the candle flame and let it burn to nothing, dropping it in your heatproof container until it burns out. Put a few drops of the oil on the flower, close your eyes, and inhale the scent. As you do, you can see whatever is making you unhappy disappearing, just as the paper turns to ash in the flames. Once you can see that in your mind, drop the flower into the dish, on top of the ash. Leave the dish on your altar as a reminder to yourself to be happy.

Winds of Change

This spell is aimed at attacking whatever causes your unhappiness. It will help to dispel any anxiety and doubts that are stopping you from being happy. For this to work, you need dried basil and dried patchouli, but you also need favorable weather. This is best done on a windy day at the top of a hill. If you don't have hills near you, find a wide-open space where it is windy. Stand in your space and turn your back to the wind. Close your eyes, focus on what is causing you unhappiness and throw the herbs up into the air. As you do, imagine your problems flying away, like the wind carrying the herbs away.

Stand still, allow the wind to flow around you, and feel each problem floating away. Say the following words:

"May the winds take my pain.

Make me happy once again.

Then turn around and face the wind. Say:

May the winds bring joy to me.

So that happy I will be"'

Weight Loss

Most of us have, at one time or another, wished we could wave a magic wand, chant a spell, and instantly melt away the excess pounds. Sadly, it just won't happen, and magic doesn't work quite that directly, especially spells for losing weight. The weight loss enchantment is powerful, but it can't work alone. The spell is merely the catalyst that lights the touch paper of your willpower and dedication. To work, you have to focus every ounce of your effort on your weight loss goals.

You must also have the willpower to draw up and stick to a diet plan, to do your daily exercises, because weight loss really isn't magic. It still requires you to burn more calories than you consume; the weight loss spells, provided you follow them carefully, will give you the push you need to be successful, to burn off that fat by sticking to your plan.

The best results come when you use your diet and your exercise regime in conjunction with at least two weight loss spells.

Melt The Pounds Away

This is a simple weight loss spell that should encourage you to stay on the course you have set for yourself. You require nothing more than a brown candle but, because this must be burning for a few nights, try to find the biggest pillar candle you can.

Take a sharp knife and inscribe your current weight onto the candle, near to the top. At the base of the candle, inscribe the weight you want to be. Do make sure you have picked a reasonable amount of weight to lose. Don't, for example, say that you want to lose 50 lbs. where it is only reasonable to expect a loss of 10 lbs. If you are reasonable in your expectations, the results are more likely to be what you want them to be.

Every night, before you go to bed, stand before your altar, and light your candle. Leave it to burn for 15 minutes and focus on your goals. As each day passes, the candle burns down, and, as it does, your own weight will begin to reduce, melting away like the candle wax.

Craving Crystal Spell

This spell can help you to beat those hunger pangs and the cravings that strike when you least expect them. It will help you to turn away from temptations that threaten to derail your good work by breaking your diet. It will keep you tied to your goals. For this spell to work, you need a green candle, some clear quartz, and, if you can get one, a green pouch or cloth bag.

The most important thing about this spell is timing. Choose a waning moon, which occurs around 14 days after the full moon. You should, if you can, cast this spell outside in the moonlight but, if not, choose a large window where you can see the moon. Light your candle, turn your face to the moon, hold the crystal, and say the following words:

"Goddess within

Goddess without

Guide me to my goal

Easy my hunger

Soothe my spirit

Strengthen my resolve

As I wish it, so mote it be."

As you say these words, close your eyes, open your mind, and focus on your goals. Focus on losing those stubborn pounds, convince yourself that you must eat a healthier diet. Think about the foods the tempt you, the unhealthy food choices you crave, and harden yourself against them. Channel the energy you create by doing this to the crystal and continue until you are set in your mind that you will not fall prey to temptation from this moment on.

When you have finished, extinguish the candle. Place the crystal in the small pouch or bag or, if you don't have one, in a pocket or bag that you carry with you all the time. Do not leave the crystal behind; where you go, the crystal goes. When you feel like temptation is in your way, grab the crystal and hold it tight. Draw on the energy it provides to put up a barrier between you and those cravings. Over time, the crystal will help you to develop the will to turn away from temptation and fight off the cravings that you might otherwise fall prey to. As time passes, the crystal will lose its energy, depending on how often you need to use it, so recharge it every month on the waning moon.

Chapter Eight: Magic and the Law of Attraction

Most people have heard of the law of attraction, but many dismiss it as utter rubbish. But it isn't rubbish; it plays a huge part in all our lives and is especially prominent in magic. When you cast a spell, you may not realize that success is largely reliant on that law of attraction, and you will see evidence of that in the results of your spell. Very often, it is the law of attraction that divides two spell casters and their successes.

When you begin to look into the law of attraction, we can see some pretty simple explanations, like your thoughts are all-powerful, and that like will attract like. What it basically means is that if you think about something long enough and often enough, it will eventually become a reality.

This works two ways – you can attract things you want, and you can attract things you don't want. It is habitual thought that attracts things to you and, if you continue to think negative thoughts all the time, all you will succeed in doing is attracting the negativity to you, all those problems and anxieties. By the same token, think positive thoughts all the time, and you will attract positivity to your life.

The law of attraction is backed up by some pretty simple, not to mention natural magic.

- What you think about the most will dictate what your reality is
- What you feel the most will dictate what your reality is
- The law of attraction is very much like the power of gravity, attracting things to you like a strong magnet
- The things you think about are the things you get
- The combination of feelings and thoughts are powerful enough to bring about change in your life

- The law of attraction is how you bring about the reality you want for the future

Thinking on that last point, you might push it aside, saying it isn't true, but it is. You already know, from your magic spells, that the universe is just one big ball of pulsating energy, all at different frequencies, and that energy also exists within you, within all of us. By using the law of attraction, you can make strong connections to the frequencies of the energy attached to what you desire, what you want.

Your thoughts are what fuels the law of attraction. When people say to you, always be careful what you think of, you should listen and avoid thinking of what you don't want. The biggest problem is that our environment and experiences affect what we think. If we are surrounded by negativity or all our experiences are tainted by negativity, then our thoughts follow suit. We tend to focus our thoughts on problems and on all the good stuff that seems to be passing us by; all that does is attract even more negativity.

We must always be aware of our thoughts; we must work at rejecting negativity by thinking only good things. This won't be easy to start with, but if we keep on doing it, we can bring about the right changes.

How to Practice The Law of Attraction

The law of attraction takes some time to understand, but you can start practicing right away; you just have to train your mind in the right way. There are some exercises you can follow to begin attracting things that we want, outcomes we believe we should have. We can break these thought processes into three separate sections – appreciation, affirmation, and then visualization. One of these alone is pretty useless; combine all three, and your results should be spectacular.

By appreciation, we are essentially referring to the feeling of gratitude. It is crucial to acknowledge the facts when things are going rather well for you in the present. By doing this, we make ourselves more aware of all the good things that happen in our lives. When we accept and acknowledge those things, we become more receptive and aware of the positivity around us. Of course, that means we focus lesser on the negativity, and that puts us in a place that allows us to see the bigger picture better.

Affirmation is basically the validation of everything we have appreciated. When we repeat the positive outcomes of the day, it makes us more aware of all the good we have done thus far. That being said, you must also be ready to reaffirm yourself when things do not go according to plan. By doing that, you are giving yourself some much-needed motivation to pick yourself back up and continue on that path against all the odds. While it may seem like a 'fake it till you make it' scenario, many have agreed that this kind of positive outlook and self-motivation have enabled them to reach heights they never thought possible.

Visualization is the easiest one because, at some point in our lives, we have all visualized something. We may have dreamed about the ideal life, the perfect house, the best situations, and so on, but all of them were just parts of the imagination running wild without any purpose other than passing the time. When channeled in tandem with appreciation and affirmation, visualization can also be a powerful tool. In addition to visualizing your dreams in vivid detail, we must also train ourselves to experience the feelings associated with achieving that dream. Once we can visualize those feelings of victor and triumph, it begins fueling the law of attraction and consequently makes our dreams come true. The law of attraction works in its primary form when one has mastered the art of using these three skills together. Such co-ordination will enable them to strengthen their magic beyond their wildest dreams.

Most spell work is built using a combination of appreciation, affirmation, and visualization. Their combined might is manifested as the energy that we witness on the physical plane. While visualization enables you to grasp a fair idea of what is expected, appreciation brings you closer to reality and affirmation rounds off the deal by having you say the spoken word that seals the deal for the enchantment. This is evident from simple spells like lighting a candle all the way up to more complex procedures.

If magic is the art of using energy to bring about the desired effect, then these three things are the tools required to channel that energy effectively. The law of attraction is the simplest way of trying to wrap our heads around the mechanics of magic.

Chapter Nine: Protection Spell

We're going to look at a couple of protection spells that can help you to protect you, and your home.

Protect Yourself

The first protection spell we're going to look at will help you to protect yourself from mental or physical harm dealt by another person. This is one of the most powerful spells you may ever perform, and it can help you throw up a shield between you and a person who won't let go of you, insisting on causing you mental anguish, and between you and other toxic people. This spell can be used to protect you from anything that could be unpleasant but, to ensure the spell remains powerful, you must repeat it several times.

One good thing is that you are not harming anyone when you cast this spell, and you are not manipulating any other person either. When you cast it, remember that you must bring as much energy out of yourself as you can, and draw as much from the earth and the sky as you can. The more energy you can draw on, the more power the spell has, and the longer it will last.

Close your eyes and visualize the person doing you harm is wrapped in a layer of shining energy, a bubble that sounds them and retains their negativity, stopping it from spreading further. That person won't even be able to expel any positive energy; if they think positive thoughts about another person, they will benefit from them and, likewise, if they think negatively about someone, wish them harm, they will be ones to reap that negativity, no-one else.

Light a candle, any color, and visualize that person standing in front of you. If you cannot do that, have a picture of them in front of you instead. Put the picture in front of your candle on the altar and then visualize the bubble around them, repeating the following multiple times:

"All negativity shall now return to you.

All negative you attempt to send me upon you will behold.

All acts, minds, and speech of hate become your own determined fate.

By all up highest, the earth and wise

By seas wide and lush blue horizons

By night and day, and powers 3

This is mine will and yes it will be.

Harm to non, nor back to me."

Protect Your Home

This next spell involves using positive energy to protect your home and, when the spell is cast, you can bring about a protective shield that surrounds your home. The spell will also help you to fix any imbalances in the energy that surrounds your home, creating a happy and harmonious place for all the people in your house.

A potent spell, its power depends on how well you focus your attention on your intent when casting it. If you are full of anger, anxiety, or feeling tired, wait; do not cast a spell at this time. Wait until your mind is calmer and not full of anxious thought jostling for space. That is the only time you should cast any spell, especially one as powerful as this.

Casting a spell is not easy at the best of times. There are guidelines and rules in place, and we mentioned them right at the start of the book. Follow them for your own safety and peace of mind. Candle spells can also be used to protect your home, and they work similarly to the spell we're going to look at in a minute. Candle spells surround your home in a warm glow, and push energy into the forces protecting your home, keeping negativity and malicious energies away.

You will need:

- A bowl, preferably one that you keep purely for spells
- A teaspoon of garlic powder or minced fresh garlic
- Coarse sea salt or coarse rock salt

Here's how you cast the protective spell:

1. Position the bowl on your altar, at the center
2. Pour the garlic and the salt into it.
3. Mix them together slowly, visualizing your house as a safe place for you and all who live there. Try to visualize the house being cloaked in a protective layer, telling yourself that negative energy cannot get through the layer.
4. When you can see your house in this way, protected from negativity, you should feel the energy leaving your body and flowing into the mix inside of the bowl
5. When you feel that energy, say the following words:

"With this salt, I cleanse this place

Let no one with ill intentions enter this space

Protect this space from all negative energies and entities

So, mote it be."

5. Now carry the mixture with you and place it on every door opening and window in your house. When you travel through your house to seal the negativity from the openings, visualize that the safe energy from the mixture is creating a shield around your house.

6. When you finish sealing the house, that is all the windows and doorways, thank the Universe for protecting you and also your home since you can live there. Let gratitude fill your body and wash away any negativity. Let the feeling of safety and warmth fill you.

Chapter Ten: Other Spells

Healing Spells

Most witches use healing spells, and these are the most commonly used after money and love spells. Most spells for health are tricky since they involve subtle influences when compared to spells used to improve one's financial situation or to find a partner. Doing magic to health, the body will not always be successful since you try to influence some physical conditions in your body. I am talking about physical healing when I say this. Healing spells are different for physical and emotional wounds. For now, let us look at some healing spells you can use for physical healing.

Power of Three

This healing spell uses the number three and the energy and strength associated with that number to heal a physical or emotional wound. This spell is best used when someone is physically ill and not when the person is injured. You can either use this spell on someone else or yourself. The latter depends on how well you can focus on the spell and yourself. The supplies you need to perform this spell are:

- Myrrh oil
- Three candles (blue, white and purple)
- Sandalwood oil
- Mint oil
- Three pieces of paper

- **Three pieces of quartz**

Smear or rub the candles with the three oils mentioned above and set them in the shape of a triangle. You need to ensure they form an equal triangle when you place them on the altar. Smear or rub the quartz stone with the oils and place one stone in front of each candle. Now, write the name of the person whom you want to heal on the piece of paper and place it in the center of the triangle. Light the candles, and while you do that, focus on the person you want to heal. Think about their health and how they would be if they were free of the symptoms. Picture their healthy self in your mind while you watch the candles burn. Now, repeat the following three times:

"Magic repair and candles burn,

Illness farewell and health come."

Let the candle burn for exactly three hours before you snuff or blow them out. The person you wanted to heal will soon show some improvement. If you want to add more power to the spell, you cast, perform this ritual three nights in a row.

The Healing Charm

Another simple spell, this has been used for thousands and thousands of years. It was used by ancient occultists as a spell to heal people who were physically ill. Casting this spell requires that you write "Abracadabra" on a sheet of paper. Then, underneath, write the word again but with one letter less. Continue until you have just the one letter left, like this:

ABRACADABRA

ABRACADABR

ABRACADAB

ABRACADA

ABRACAD

ABRACA

ABRAC

ABRA

ABR

AB

A

Roll up the piece of paper as small as you can and place it in a pendant or small vial; wear it on a chain around your neck, and the belief is that the disease symptoms will gradually disappear in the same way as the letters in the word did.

Candle Spells

Spells to Reunite Lovers

These spells are designed to help you rekindle the spark, to bring romance back into your relationship. Many witches choose these spells when they are separated from their loved ones because of work, school, meetings, and other circumstances. However, they can also be used to bring lovers back together after a relationship has broken up. There are other spells you can use in these circumstances as well, and we saw some of those in another part of the book.

Candle Melding Love Spell

When the candles begin to melt, and the wax melds together, you and your partner will be drawn to one another once more.

You will need

- 2 red candles that are shaped like humans
- Some ginger oil

If you can't find any red candles shaped as figures, just use standard candles, so long as they are red. Smear the ginger oil over both candles and then place them in a dish together. They must be in the same dish, not in separate ones, as the candles have to be touching.

Light both candles and focus on positive thoughts of your partner as the wax begins melting. Let the wax from the candles run into each other and focus on the spell and your partner until the candles are sufficiently melted to join together. Repeat the following words until you feel you have got your message across to the universe.

"Candles burn, and wax will run

You and I again are one."

Leave the candles to burn out by themselves.

Return to Me Candle Spell

This is another powerful spell that can help you and your partner reunite.

You will need

- Some red yarn or string
- Some vanilla oil
- One candle, either red, white, or pink

Inscribe the candle with your initials or your full name using a sharp implement. Above yours, in the center of the candle, inscribe your partner's name or initials, ensuring you write over the top of the first letters.

Smear oil on the candle and then tie the red yarn around it. Tie it in a bow, making sure the knot is above the initials. Light it and leave it to burn until the flame is getting close to the top carving. Extinguish the candle and leave it near to your altar, letting the universe know that your spell will be completed when your partner has returned to you. Every day, rub more oil over the initials, only stopping when you are reunited.

Flames of Progress

This is a spell designed to help you progress in whatever you want to move forward in, particularly if you find yourself at a sticking point along the road of your life. You may be facing issues such as relationship problems or money worries, and if you can't seem to find a way forward or you've simply lost the motivation to get on, this spell can help you. It can help to give you the motivation you need to help you make improvements in whatever you use the spell for.

You will need

- 3 candles – one white, one dark blue, and one pale blue
- A sharp implement – knife, pin, pen, etc.
- A cinnamon incense stick

Before you start, take the candles, and carve these runes into them:

- Around the center of the white candle, carve the Thurisaz rune
- Around the center of the pale blue candle, carve the Raidho rune
- Around the center of the dark blue candle, carve the Jera rune.

Now put each candle into a holder of its own and place the white candle to the left of you, the dark blue to the right, and the pale blue once in the center.

Take hold of your cinnamon incense stick and focus your attention on whatever issues are troubling you. The incense should be held in your dominant hand. Light it and then, using the flame from the incense, light the white candle. Extinguish the incense and put it into another holder. Say these words aloud:

"With this flame, the spell is lit.

I need to move, not to sit."

Light the pale blue candle in the center with the flame from the white candle and say these words:

"With this flame, the spell goes on.

As of now, the delay is gone."

Lastly, use the pale blue candle to light the dark blue candle and say these words to finish the spell:

"With this flame, the spell is cast.

Things will start to move at last."

Look at each of the candles in turn and say the words again in the same order The candles should remain on your altar and be left to go out by themselves, and you should soon start to see things changing in your life.

The Light of Three

This is sometimes used as a kind of dream spell. If you have questions you need answering, it can bring you those answers in the form of a dream.

You will need

- A piece of amethyst or a whole amethyst crystal
- A candle with three wicks
- A jar
- Some sandalwood oil
- Some dried mugwort

Three-wick candles are readily available in any home décor stores, even though they are not a common household candle. Lavender is the best color if you can get it; if not, go for a white one.

Focus your attention on the question you want to be answered and keep it focused throughout the whole spell.

Sprinkle a little dried Mugwort on the surface of the candle. Rub some sandalwood oil over the amethyst. Touch the crystal three times to your forehead, forming a triangular shape as you do. Focus and ask the universe to assist you in opening your third eye.

Now put the crystal onto the candle, positioned in the center of the three wicks. Hold your palm over the top of the candle and voice your question aloud. Light all three wicks and ask the question once more. Leave the candle to burn out by itself, and then, over the next few days, note what you experience in your dreams. If a symbol or a pattern stands out or recurs, that is the answer you are seeking.

Healing Friendships and Relationships

Lots of people think about love spells, about casting spells to make a person fall for them or to stop doing something they should not be doing. There are much better ways that you can achieve this. It isn't always about control and, when things start to get tough, you don't need to be in control of another person – that can often make things much worse. Ask yourself a question – do you have control over the way you respond to a situation? If not, how can you take control? Before you respond to anything, take a bit of time to reflect and ask these questions:

- Is having control over someone unhealthy? Unethical? Is control the only way to deal with a situation?
- If the person involved could understand that their actions affected you, and how, do you think their behavior would be any different?
- If you could understand why the person behaved in that way, could you more easily accept what they have done? Perhaps try to help them?
- Think about your actions – do they have an effect on how that person behaves?

When it comes to healing, to building bridges in friendships or relationships, control is never the answer; instead, you should be looking for a way to see that person in a different light. There's an old saying, "It takes two to tango," and this is very true. It means that both of you should take responsibility for the argument or the upset in your relationship, and it's down to both of you to try to make peace.

To do that, a spell is required, a spell that will help them to see that you are not their enemy. A spell to help bring about better understanding and more love. While you can make a change to how you respond to a person, you can only do it effectively if you understand why they are acting as they are.

For the spell, you will need

- A light blue candle
- Some dried sage
- Some dried catnip
- Some jasmine oil

Take a piece of paper and write down the name of the person. Add a + symbol and then write your own name. Rub the jasmine oil over the candle and then sprinkle dried catnip and dried sage over it. Light the candle, saying the following words as you do so:

"I cannot force you to behave,

A good friendship [or relationship] is what I crave,

A unity of peace and mutual respect,

A showing of love in every aspect.

I call to the unending wisdom of Danu,

To give me insight on just how to reach you,

To question my motives, and search for the good,

To look beyond flaws, so you feel understood,

To open your eyes too, so you understand,

That a love worth having is worth fighting for,

That you cherish those that love you and love them back more."

Light the candle and burn it every night before bed, just for a few minutes. Always remember to put the candle out before you go to sleep – do not blow it out as you can upset the elements; instead, snuff it out.

Reuniting The Reflections Spell

The reuniting spell uses a mirror, divining the power from it to help you and a loved one reunite.

You will need

- Some paper made from fine linen
- A pen
- A mirror
- A piece of each of the following crystals – red jasper, rose quartz, garnet, and carnelian

Write down your name on the linen paper, making sure to write your full name – no nicknames! Underneath your name, write down the name of the person you want to reunite with.

Place the paper, so it is facing the mirror glass and is reflected in it. Move the mirror slightly, just so that it is facing but not resting on the paper. The best type of mirror is a makeup mirror that has a tilting stand.

Scatter the crystals over your names on the paper and say these words several times:

"Mirror, mirror, do you see?

Bring my lover back to me."

Soon, you will hear that the person you miss so much is coming back.

You must keep in mind that this spell can only work if the person you want to reunite with has loved you at some point or still does.

If you are trying to force a person to fall for you, then you are wandering into the realms of black magic, because you are attempting to take control of their emotions. That is not Wicca; that isn't what it's all about.

Safe Revenge Spell

Sometimes, if someone has caused you hurt, you want them to know how much they have hurt you; you want them to understand how their actions have affected you. This doesn't give you permission to dive into using black magic, not at all. There are some safe spells that you can use to help that person understand the effect they had on you.

First, focus on the person who caused you the hurt. Make a mental list of all their shortcomings. Next, consider their higher being and mentally list all the reasons they struggle to live up to that being – how they struggle and why.

Think about a positive quality that you would like this person to have. You do this, so your spell doesn't cause their lives any damage. Let's say, for example, that you want payback for a drug dealer, perhaps because you know he sells to young people, or he forces people to do his dealing for him. That positive quality could be a conscience. That might make it hard for them to sell their drugs in the future because, all of a sudden, that conscience kicks in and stops them. You could also request that the universe opens their heart, so they can see the people around them, understand them and even, maybe, love them.

When you ask for a positive quality from the universe, choose from these:

- Clarity
- Connection to a higher source of spirituality
- Enlightenment
- Freedom
- Honor

- Intelligence

- Love

- Opening the heart and the soul

- Understanding

- Vision

All of these qualities will affect the way the recipient behaves. The badness that surrounds their identity will break apart, and they begin to hurt, to suffer as they have made others suffer. If any one of these qualities came back at you threefold, think of how much you would gain! You would gain in these three primary ways:

- You get to take revenge on a person who has ignored his higher calling and not lived up to his higher being
- When it comes to their higher being, you get to do the right thing
- As a bonus, what you send out to the universe, you get back, In other words, you reap what you sow

To do this spell:

Light a candle (any candle) and sit before it. Call on the person you are focused on and then call on his higher being. Ask his higher being what the best quality would be to ask for so that you can be instrumental in bringing about change in their lives.

Say the positive quality out loud and read these words:

"Upon the planes in which I live,

The gift of [insert quality] I now give,

To [insert the name of the revenge target] with all my heart and soul,

To change [him/her] and to make [him/her] whole;

By all on high and law of three,

This is my will, so shall it be."

Visualize that person in the flames of the candle, just for a few minutes, and then extinguish the candle. You have completed the spell, and now, you can sit back and wait for it to take effect.

Find a New Job

Either write your own job advertisement or find the job you want to apply for. For this spell to work, you must create an ideal situation for yourself and visualize it. Therefore, you must be specific about the location, job, and salary. You can also add more details to your visualization if needed since the effect of the spell is greater when you add more details; however, you should be realistic. Do not expect too much of the Universe. For this spell, you need to light a large deep blue candle. Blue represents the planet Jupiter, and most witches perform rituals to worship Jupiter when they need jobs. Place the lit candle on a metal tray.

Now, read the advertisement you created or read numerous times and fold the paper into a cone. Burn the paper over the flame and let the ash from the paper fall into the tray. Once the paper is fully burned, collect the ashes and place them in a bag or box. If the candle goes out, do not worry too much. Light the candle again. Let the Universe know you are persistent and want to get the job.

Bury the bag or box with the ashes under an oak, ash, or another energy tree close to the place you want to work. If there is no such tree around the area, bury the ashes in a flowerpot, preferably one with a peppermint plant since peppermint is an energizer. This is when your ritual comes to an end. The most important part of this spell is to get a job, so you cannot forget this step.

Now, end the magic spell. You will see the results in some time, but this does not mean you stop looking for a job. Always be attentive and grab opportunities that work for you.

Find Your Dream Job

You should cast this spell only after you send the application or resume to the employer. Use a sharp knife or [in to write the name of the company where you want to work on a large green candle. Take a red candle and carve the victory rune, also known as Tiwaz. This rune looks like an upward pointing arrow. Write your full name under the rune.

Burn these candles for 30 minutes after the sunsets on Thursday, and visualize yourself getting the job you so badly want. After 30 minutes, snuff the candle out. Do not blow out the candles. Wet your fingers and put out the candles. Now, use the same candles every Thursday and watch them burn for 15 minutes while you visualize yourself getting the job. Do this until the candles until you get a job, or they are fully extinguished. Throw the candles away and leave a small bowl of milk at night after you get the job. This is a way to say thanks.

Chapter Eleven: Crystals and Magic

When you perform any magic, using crystal energy, you need to ensure you choose the right crystals for yourself. To do this, you must use your intuition to help you identify the right crystal for you. Crystals are often used in Wicca to direct energy towards different objects. They can also be used to store energy collected during a ritual or spell for safekeeping. Therefore, it is important that you choose the right crystal when you perform any ritual or cast a spell using a crystal.

Crystals have a special ability to store or emit energy, and every crystal has a different vibration or frequency. You can use the energy in the crystals to help you overcome various issues in life. You can also increase the intensity of the spells you cast using crystals. The crystals are better than regular rocks, and all have a geometric pattern, which is the reason behind the energy in the crystals. These geometric patterns are more intricate than the cell structure in the human body. Before we look at different methods to choose a crystal, let us look at some crystal types.

Types

Clear Quartz

This is the best crystal to use for healing. This has no negative effects whatsoever but needs to be cleansed before you use it. You can use the energy in this crystal to clear different types of energies in your body – physical, mental, spiritual, and emotional. You can align the energy in the chakras and your aura. This crystal can be cleaned easily. You will find it very easy to program the crystal, which will help you balance all the energies in your body. You can create a great impression on your soul.

Onyx

This crystal helps to balance opposing forces of energy – the yin and the yang. You can reduce any form of stress in your body when you use this crystal. You can exercise a good level of self-control and will find happiness in the smallest things. Good fortune becomes your very good friend.

Opal

The opal crystal is a brilliant one since it works on improving all your attributes. You can enhance your creativity and imagination. A student would love this crystal since he or she would be able to improve his memory, which would prove beneficial for them during the examinations. It also helps to remove any inhibitions you may have.

Moonstone

This is a crystal that is often used by women since it always keeps them calm during pregnancy and the menstrual cycle. The energy is always balanced, and so are the thoughts in mind. It is because of this crystal that clairvoyants find their capabilities increasing and sharpening. You can balance certain areas in your body using this crystal. You can keep any negative emotions at bay. The moonstone crystal helps to stimulate confidence in you and will balance all your feelings and emotions. You can perceive things around you much better than you ever had. A woman will benefit from using this crystal since it enhances the feminine nature.

Rose Quartz

This crystal is one that depicts every aspect of love. You can use this crystal to cast various love spells. This crystal helps you understand your desires and emotions better and can understand all your feelings. You can increase your trust and faith in the people around you. You can love yourself unconditionally, which will help to introduce you to your inner self. You can remove any depression and grief. The love that you have for yourself will help you overcome any negative thoughts you may have about yourself. Any resentment that you feel towards the people around you will vanish when you use this crystal. The best combination of this crystal is amethyst.

Moss Agate

It is also known as Dendritic Agate or tree Agate. It is a semi-opaque stone with wisps of white and green that resembles Moss and hence its name. These stones are used for their protective and healing abilities. Moss Agate is believed to help strengthen one's connection with the elements- earth.

Red Goldstone

It is also known as red sandstone, and it is essentially a bright orange-red colored gem with specks of gold. It is associated with the sacred chakra and promotes creativity, drive, and confidence in the wearer. Red sandstone is formed when copper salts are added to molten glass.

Rudraksha Seeds

Rudraksha is not a crystal or a stone, but it is worth learning more about this seed. A rudraksha seed is believed to have miraculous powers. This seed is important in Hinduism, and numerous scriptures, including the Vedas, talk about how these seeds benefit the human race. According to Hindu mythology, these seeds were created from the tears shed by Lord Shiva. You can wear a seed around your neck if you think someone is using black magic against you.

Turquoise

Turquoise is a blue-green stone that is beautiful to look at. This stone has many healing properties, and it is believed that it is a key to the door between earth and heaven. The energy in this stone will help you connect with the energy in the universe. Many Native American tribes believe that this stone helps people reach enlightenment. Chinese healers also use this stone in their native healing rituals. This stone is associated with the throat chakra. If there are any imbalances in the throat chakra, they can be removed using this stone.

Prehnite

This stone is yellow-green in color and can be either translucent or opaque. It contains little specks of black rutile present in it. It is quite popular among healers and wisdom seekers. It is believed that this stone gives the strength that's necessary for facing the realities of life with grace and patience. This stone is also associated with the heart chakra and helps remove any negative energy, which is stagnant and one's body because of any old injuries or grievances. Empaths often use it because it can heal the healers. This stone helps strengthen one's feelings of empathy.

Choosing the Right Crystal

Now that you are aware of the different crystals and also their significance, you must learn how to select the right crystals for you. Remember that different crystals have different effects on your body, and the crystals that work for another person may not necessarily work for you. You can choose the crystals for yourself based on the trial and error method. This section will discuss different techniques you can use to determine which crystal is right for you.

Call Upon the Crystal

When you choose a crystal for yourself, call upon the energies in the universe to assess whether a specific crystal will work for you or not. You can ask the universe to send you signs and help you choose the right crystals for you. When you do this, you can choose the right crystals since you know the Universe will not lead you astray. You should remember to keep an open mind and receive the energy from the crystal.

Physical Reaction

Every crystal has a specific energy, and one of the easiest ways to determine if a crystal is right for you or not is to place your non-dominant hand over the crystal. If the energy in the crystal calls towards your hand, then this is the right crystal for you. You can use this crystal to perform different spells. If you want to select healing stones, hold the crystal in your hand, and feel the energy within the crystal. Pay attention to how your body reacts to the energy in the crystal. Close your eyes, and pay attention to the sensation in your hand. Start working with your non-dominant hand and then move the crystal to your dominant hand.

Different Properties

If you know that there are specific wants that you want to address using a crystal, make a list of those wants. When you have the list, make a list of the crystals that will help you fulfill those needs. One of the best ways to do this is to look for a crystal that will heal a chakra or a specific part of your body. As mentioned earlier, there are seven chakras in the body, and each of these chakras is associated with different colors. For example, if you want to heal the root chakra, you should look for a red-colored crystal. Read through the sections above to associate a color with each chakra in your body. Different crystals are also associated with different elements. If you want to work with a specific element, you should use the crystal associated with that element.

Cleansing and Clearing

You should clean the crystals well if you want to maintain the energy within the crystals. So, make sure you cleanse the crystals, especially if you use them frequently or have not used them in a while. Cleanse the crystals when you purchase them and also every few days after you use them. Since crystals store energy, they may also absorb some negative energy during a spell. This will only damage the crystal and render it useless to you. One of the easiest ways to cleanse a crystal is to place it either in moonlight or sunlight. You should let the natural light course through your crystal and clean the energy within the crystal.

Research

Understand the different types of crystals you can use to cast various spells and perform rituals. Purchase a crystal only when you know and understand its properties.

Purpose

It is also important to know why you want to use a specific crystal. It is only when you understand that you can choose the right crystal. You will need to choose small stones if you want to use a crystal in jewelry. If you want to use them during meditation, you should use medium-sized crystals. You can use large crystals if you want to use them to cleanse other crystals you are using. Keep the following questions in mind when you want to identify the purpose:

1. How do you want to use the crystals?

2. Where do you want to place the crystals?

3. What spells do you want to cast using the crystals?

4. Do you want only to cast love spells?

When you answer these questions, you will know which crystal you want to purchase for yourself.

Rituals

Motivational Ritual

If you need Monday motivation and find it hard to get out of bed to get to work, why not try the quick motivation ritual? You can get your work done like a boss when you perform this ritual. To perform this ritual, you need red jasper. This crystal is grounded and is the perfect stone to help you get down to business. The stone's energy encourages you and supports you.

Hold the crystal in the palm of your dominant hand, and focus on the energy in the crystal. Now, let the energy in the crystal guide you towards the areas you need to improve. When you hold onto the stone, ask yourself what areas in your life you need to take action in, and listen to the stone tell you what you must do.

Creativity Ritual

Since creativity benefits people in every area of life, regardless of whether it is a relationship, art practice, work, or even your picture grid on Instagram, it is important to let the creative juices flow. You can use the energy from different crystals to open your creative channel and let yourself feel more inspired and original. To perform this ritual, you must use a carnelian. This crystal is a powerful stone and calls the creative energy situated in your sacral chakra.

Hold the crystal in the palm of your dominant hand, and say the following words aloud, "I am creative." These words hold immense power, and their intent is enhanced by the energy in the crystal.

Chapter Twelve: Wicca Herbal Magic

Since the plant kingdom developed on Earth well before human beings evolved, you can say that herbs are one of the oldest magical objects or tools that exist. Plants have many properties that help people maintain both spiritual and physical wellbeing. When healers, medicine men, and shamans incorporated different species of plants into their practices, herbal magic began to gain popularity. Before magic was separated from medicine, people used to accompany physical healing with prayer and ritual. They used an herbal tea or concoction and performed a ritual or repeated an incantation for a speedy recovery. People now know that a cup of herbal tea has both spiritual and emotional effects and also has nutritional effects and benefits for people. Since herbs are used for their magical healing properties, people who cast spells must learn more about herbal magic, and learn about the different herbs they can use when they cast spells.

Elemental Power of Plants

When it comes to the various symbols used in magic, plants embody or signify the power of the four elements working together. Since plants begin as seeds in the soil, they need minerals and vitamins to sustain. They also interact with sunlight, which acts as a catalyst to convert carbon dioxide into oxygen. This directly affects the air quality around the plant. The air around the plant can foster more life in the environment through the wind. Wind stimulates the growth of leaves and stems. It also scatters seeds between plants to continue the cycle of growth. Since plants also need some water to live, they play a crucial role in the regulation of the water cycle. They help to purify water and move it from the soil into the atmosphere. It is for this reason; spell casters use plants or herbs to enhance the strength of the energy used during a ritual. Plants represent how the four elements work together.

Plant Intelligence

The famous Greek philosopher, Aristotle, believed that even plants have psyches, and many witches or Wiccans believe the same. Psyche is a word used to describe the human spirit or soul. Scientists also have found evidence to prove that plants do have a certain level of consciousness. Research shows that plants can feel pain.

It is known that plants communicate and cooperate with various beings in the wild and with other plants. They also cooperate with different plant species. Consider a forest setting. In this setting, every shrub, tree and plant exchanges information with each other using an underground network of fungi and roads. This network allows various plants to exchange minerals and vitamins with each other and help each other by making up for any shortages during the growing phase. This is similar to you borrowing eggs or sugar from a neighbor and returning the favor in the future with a little extra butter or cake. For instance, if an insect bites a flower or leaf, the plant releases various chemicals to repel the insect. These chemicals act as a stimulus and prompt the neighboring plants to release the chemicals to repel the same insects.

These discoveries help people understand a plant's intelligence. Regardless of whether you work with the plant seeds, roots, leaves, stems, berries, or flowers, you can tap into this magical energy when you use herbs in your practice.

Versatile and Hand-On Magic

It is good to work with plants or herbs from your own magical garden, especially if you want to connect with the energies present in the earth. When you harvest and grow herbs in your garden, you are in touch with various energies in the Earth, including rain, wind, sun, and the energy of the various insects and animal life. What is more is that when you garden, you can charge various tools you use with your energy. You also transfer some of your energy into the soil, which means your energy is used as part of the various life and death cycles taking place in the garden.

Herbs are the most versatile magical objects or tools you can use when you cast spells or perform rituals. You can use herbs to create various magical crafts, such as puppets, spell jars, dream pillows, sachets, and other objects. Some practitioners also create their own oils and incense using herbs, and these add more power to their spell work. Herbs can also be used in the kitchen. You can create magical tinctures, baked goods, potions, teas, and other foods and beverages using herbs. Most practitioners use herbs in different forms of spell work, right from candle magic to bath spells. Some spells require the caster to smudge the dried herbs or use dried herbs to remove any negative energy before they perform any ritual or cast a spell.

Some practitioners also use specific herbs to mark the protective circle before they begin their Sabbat rituals. There are some who also use specific herbs to honor their deities or natural elements, such as lemon balm or lavender. The former is sacred to Diana, the Roman goddess. Herbal magic is practical, and most of it can be done with various ingredients that you already have in your kitchen.

What is an Herb?

There are various characteristics that separate herbs from other plants in the plant kingdom. For cooks, Witches, and healers, an herb can be anything that is useful to people. They may use herbs for the following purposes:

- `Medicine`
- `To add fragrance`
- `In cooking`
- `Clothing`
- `Spiritual and magical work`

Trees and shrubs are also included in the list of herbs. You can also include vegetables, fruit, flowers, grass, and other plants that some cultures or traditions believe are weeds.

It is important to note that for both herbalists and Witches, an herb is a plant that benefits the body. Herbs can also include toxic plants, such as henbane and belladonna. People who understand herbs know that no plant is good or bad. Every plant has its own specific uses, especially when it comes to the human body. If you are only starting with herbal magic, ensure that you follow all warnings about toxic herbs. Listen to what experts have to say about herbs, and remember it is better to be safe than sorry. Always look for non-toxic substitutes when you cast spells.

How to Get Started with Herbal Magic

There is a lot of information available about herbal magic, and it can be overwhelming when you first read about it. You, however, do not have to be a master at botany or a gardener to begin your practice. All you must do is to acquaint yourself with some of the herbs. One of the best ways to build a relationship with the energy in the plant world is to spend some time with the herbs.

Most herbs used in magic can be found in the spice section at the supermarket. If you are starting out with Wicca, try some simple herbal spells and begin casting complex ones as you gradually build your knowledge.

Conclusion

Wicca is a practice of witchcraft and spell work, and there are only a few who completely understand what this tradition or practice is. Most people worry that this practice is based on lies since there are quite a few people out there who do not believe in magic or witchcraft.

Wicca is traditionally practiced in Western culture, and the practitioners use energy from the natural elements and other beings to perform their rituals or cast spells. The Wiccan tradition is based on the principle of never causing harm to another individual. That said, it is hard to determine what harm is since it is a relative concept, but Wiccans must never willfully harm another being, especially when they cast a spell.

Most spells in the Wiccan tradition are based on white magic, and this magic is pure and does not cause harm to another being. There are other forms of magic, namely red and black magic, that are considered evil, and only some witches perform such magic. This book sheds some light on the different forms of magic to help understand more about Wicca. Since Wicca is based on white magic, any spell you cast does not affect another individual.

Most people avoided discussing Wicca and Witchcraft until the early 1950s when Gerald Gardner began to talk about magic and witchcraft. He had also set up a coven, known as the Bricket Wood Coven, and was the High Priest. Soon Doreen Valiente joined Gardner as the High Priestess, and the two of them rewrote the Book of Shadows. This book had all the information a Witch needed about the craft and also some common practices that Wiccans need to adhere to.

If you are new to the practice of Wicca, you may have many questions about tradition and culture. This book provides all the information you need about the practice. The book starts off by explaining what Wicca is, and the various aspects of Wicca. It also talks about how Wicca has obtained some traditions and cultures from occult practices. The book also sheds some light on how Gerald Gardner, known as the Father of Wicca, used some principles of Occult to set the framework for Wicca.

The book also tells you about the different methods you need to follow when you cast your first spell or perform your ritual. If you are a novice, you must first learn various tips and tricks to help you cast spells successfully. Since you use your energy and energy from other sources, such as the objects placed on the altar, you need to ensure you create a protective circle around yourself to prevent the influence of any negative energy. The book also tells you what you must do to create a protective circle around you, and how you should come out of the circle after you perform a ritual or cast a spell.

As mentioned earlier, Wiccan practitioners use white magic to cast their spells since they do not want to harm anybody. There are, however, other forms of magic known as red and black magic. These forms of magic are considered dark or negative forms of magic since the objective is the harm another individual or use their energy force to cast the spell. A ritual or practice of Wicca known as sex magic is also considered red magic, but this depends on your intentions. If you cast a spell using sex magic with the permission of your partner, then you are not causing anybody harm. Both of you are working towards the same intent, giving a stronger chance of that intent manifesting itself in the world.

Any form of magic is only as strong as the spell caster's intent, and if you want to cast the right spells and manifest your intent in the world, use the energy within yourself and in the objects in your altar to intensity the intent. This book also leaves you with different spells you can use to attract love, money, and prosperity. It also sheds some light on different protection and healing spells you can use to safeguard yourself, your home, and the people you love.

Since Wicca allows the use of different objects, people tend to use crystals and herbs to intensify or enhance their intent. They also use these objects to perform rituals and spells. This book also provides information on herbal magic and crystal magic. You learn how to choose the right crystal and also perform simple rituals to improve your creativity.

If you are a novice, you can use this book as your guide. It has all the information you need about Wicca and helps you cast the right spells. It will teach you the different traditions and rules you must follow when you cast spells or perform any ritual.

Thanks for Reading

What did you think of, **Wicca: This Book Includes: Wicca For Beginners & Wicca Spells. Discover The Power of Wicca, Wiccan Spells, Herbal Magic, Essential Oils & Witchcraft Rituals?**

I know you could have picked any number of books to read, but you picked this book and for that I am extremely grateful.

I hope that it added at value and quality to your everyday life. If so, it would be really nice if you could share this book with your friends and family.

If you enjoyed this book and found some benefit in reading this, I'd like to hear from you and hope that you could take some time to post a review. Your feedback and support will help this author to greatly improve his writing craft for future projects and make this book even better.

I want you, the reader, to know that your review is very important and so, if you'd like to leave a review, all you have to do is click here and away you go. I wish you all the best in your future success!

Thank you and good luck

Sofia Visconti

A SPIRITUAL START!

Start your week with gratitude, joy, inspiration, and love.

Healing, motivation, inspiration, challenge and guidance straight to your inbox every week!

FIND OUT MORE

Resources

https://Wiccanow.com/home-protection-spell/

https://wiccaliving.com/law-of-attraction/

https://samanthamarswriter.blogspot.com/2013/01/protection-spell.html

https://www.free-witchcraft-spells.com/wellbeing-spells.html

https://www.free-witchcraft-spells.com/weight-loss-spells.html

https://www.free-witchcraft-spells.com/energy-spells.html

https://www.free-witchcraft-spells.com/happiness-spells.html

https://hubpages.com/religion-philosophy/Top-5-Money-Attraction-Rituals

https://wiccaliving.com/wheel-of-the-year-Wiccan-sabbats/

https://www.wikihow.com/Do-White-Magic

https://www.womenofgrace.com/blog/?p=55059

https://isha.sadhguru.org/in/en/wisdom/article/black-magic

https://witchcraftway.com/spells/love-spells/a-red-candle-love-spell/

https://www.cosmopolitan.com/sex-love/a31994289/how-to-do-a-love-spell/

https://www.allure.com/story/how-to-cast-love-spells

https://www.llewellyn.com/spell.php?spell_id=7022

https://moodymoons.com/2019/08/12/love-goddess-spell-poppet-tutorial/

https://www.free-witchcraft-spells.com/healing-spells.html

https://www.free-witchcraft-spells.com/free-easy-love-spells.html

https://www.free-witchcraft-spells.com/white-magic-love-spells.html

https://www.free-witchcraft-spells.com/free-money-spells.html

https://www.free-witchcraft-spells.com/free-spells-for-money.html

https://www.free-witchcraft-spells.com/candle-spells.html

https://www.free-witchcraft-spells.com/reunite-lovers-spells.html

https://www.free-witchcraft-spells.com/free-candle-spells.html

https://www.free-witchcraft-spells.com/easy-magic-spells.html

https://www.wattpad.com/594502699-Wiccan-witchcraft-spells-and-information

https://wiccaliving.com/beginners-guide-herbal-magic/

https://magic-spells-and-potions.com/safe_revenge_spell.htm

https://lovemagicworks.com/get-job/

Printed in Great Britain
by Amazon